The Amish

Young Center Books in Anabaptist
and Pietist Studies

Donald B. Kraybill, *Series Editor*

THE AMISH

A Concise Introduction

Steven M. Nolt

JOHNS HOPKINS UNIVERSITY PRESS   *Baltimore*

Johns Hopkins University Press
2715 North Charles Street
Baltimore, Maryland 21218-4363
www.press.jhu.edu

Library of Congress Cataloging-in-Publication Data

Nolt, Steven M., 1968– author.
The Amish : a concise introduction / Steven M. Nolt.
pages cm. — (Young Center books in Anabaptist
and Pietist studies)
Includes bibliographical references and index.
ISBN 978-1-4214-1956-5 (pbk. : alk. paper) — ISBN 1-4214-1956-4
(pbk. : alk. paper) — ISBN 978-1-4214-1957-2 (electronic) —
ISBN 1-4214-1957-2 (electronic)
1. Amish—United States—Social life and customs.
2. Amish—History. I. Title.
E184.M45.N65 2016
289.7′3—dc23   2015028198

A catalog record for this book is available from the British Library.

*Special discounts are available for bulk purchases of this book. For more
information, please contact Special Sales at 410-516-6936 or
specialsales@press.jhu.edu.*

Contents

THE AMISH

CHAPTER ONE

Meet the Amish

In 2013 an Amish father placed a notice in an Amish newspaper for a meeting of parents and teachers involved with Amish schools. Information about the gathering, to be held in Punxsutawney, Pennsylvania, ended with this reminder: "If you are planning to attend and are using a GPS, you must use the correct spelling [for Punxsutawney]."[1]

The Amish use global positioning systems?

For many Americans, the image of the Amish as reclusive, dark-clad, horse-and-buggy-driving folks conjures notions of the nineteenth century and hardly comports with twenty-first-century satellite technology. In fact, most observers would either be perplexed by the notice or decide that it reveals some secret hypocrisy among a people who present a publicly plain life but behind the scenes are actually no different from the rest of us.

The truth is something else, as we will see, but the Punxsutawney school meeting lays bare distinctive aspects of

Amish life in the modern world. None of the Amish reading the announcement has a driver's license. All of them rely on horse-drawn transportation for local errands. But for longer trips, most Amish families turn to non-Amish neighbors, hiring them to act as informal taxis. And many of *those* drivers rely on GPS, which the Amish recognize and understand.

That sort of give and take—refusing to own a car but hiring outside drivers and being aware of what those drivers want and expect—reveals the dynamic Amish relationship with the wider world that we'll explore in this book. The Amish are a separate people, to be sure, but they are not as socially or technologically isolated as we often imagine. Instead, they interact with the wider world by bargaining with modernity.[2] The Amish participate in modern life on their own terms. They might use batteries, for example, but not electricity from the public grid. While such choices may seem confusing from an outside perspective, this sort of flexible negotiating with the forces of modern life has allowed them to flourish.

Yet the Amish give-and-take extends only so far. The Punxsutawney meeting brought together Amish parents and teachers from across western Pennsylvania to discuss the day-to-day operations of Amish schools. Across the country some two thousand one- and two-room Amish schools exist in silent testimony to the refusal of parents to bow to the demands and promises of modern modes of education. Amish schools educate children only through the eighth grade, use a curriculum from the early 1900s, and employ teachers who themselves have had only eight years of schooling. During the 1950s and 1960s hundreds of Amish parents went to prison rather than send their offspring to consolidated public schools or to high schools of any kind. Their refusal to budge on this issue ultimately landed them before the U.S. Supreme Court, which in the case *Wisconsin v. Yoder* (1972) affirmed the Amish dissent from mass education and contributed to the jurisprudence of American religious liberty and minority rights.

Combining a stubborn commitment to old-fashioned education with knowledge of GPS and the flexibility to hire drivers who use such systems, the meeting in Punxsutawney embodies aspects of Amish life that intrigue and perplex the rest of us.

An Amish woman loads her grocery purchases into a cargo van driven by a non-Amish neighbor who brought her to town. *Credit: Joel Fath/Mennonite Historical Library*

Amish Myths

Popular images of the Amish sometimes resolve the puzzling aspects of Amish life with simplistic half-truths or outright misconceptions. These myths stem, understandably, from the potentially confusing diversity of Amish customs, as well as from the fact that the multi-million-dollar Amish-themed tourism industry (dominated by non-Amish players) sometimes offers up highly romanticized images of Amish life. And some of the misinformation derives from intentionally skewed presentations of Amish society that appear in reality television or Amish-themed fiction geared toward public entertainment.

Myths about the Amish include:

- The Amish are shut off from meaningful interaction with the wider world. They live in isolated colonies and shun all outsiders.
- The Amish are Luddites who live without technology and reject all modern conveniences. If you see an Amish contractor using a cell phone or an Amish teenager with in-line skates, they are acting on the sly and would be severely punished if Amish leaders caught them.
- Amish don't pay taxes or use modern medicine. They rely on mafia-style gangs to maintain order and they have very high rates of genetic abnormalities due to "inbreeding."
- All Amish are farmers. They grow or hand-make nearly everything they use and rarely shop in stores.
- At age sixteen Amish children are sent out into the world to explore life in big cities before deciding if they want to come back home.
- Amish people have few choices in life. Bishops within the Amish church make all the decisions and women, especially, simply do as they are told.
- The Amish may live a bit differently than the rest of us, but they share the same basic cultural assumptions that the rest of us do and they represent the best of traditional American values.
- As relics from another age, the Amish are slowly but surely dying out.

Amish Reality: Diversity and Commonality

In the chapters that follow we unpack these and other misconceptions about Amish life, but for now we'll look at the last one—the idea that the Amish are a dying breed. In fact, the Amish population is growing rapidly, doubling about every eighteen to twenty years. Today more than 300,000 Amish people—adults and children— live in the United States and eastern Canada. The largest Amish

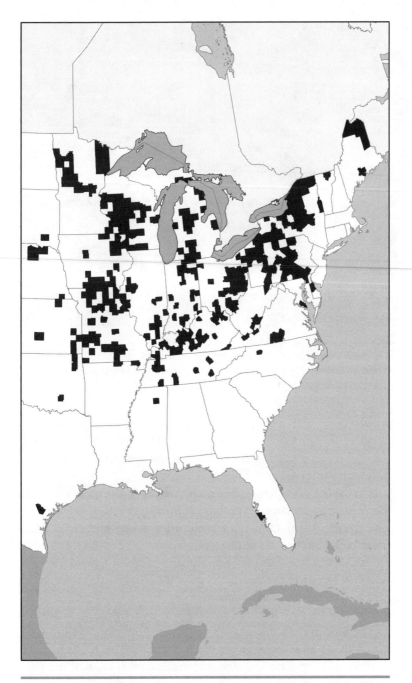

Fig. 1.1. Counties in the United States with Amish Communities in 2015. There are also small numbers of Amish in Colorado, Idaho, Montana, South Dakota, and Wyoming. In addition, there are sixteen Amish settlements in the Canadian province of Ontario and one in New Brunswick. *Map prepared by St. Lawrence University Libraries GIS Program*

The Amish population is growing rapidly, fueled by large families and the fact that the vast majority of Amish children choose to join their parents' church. *Credit: Don Burke*

populations are in Ohio, Pennsylvania, and Indiana, but growing numbers live in Wisconsin, New York, Michigan, Missouri, and Kentucky, and smaller communities are scattered from Montana to Maine and from Texas to Florida.[3]

On the one hand, there is no mystery behind Amish growth. Amish families are much larger than those of mainstream U.S. households. The average Amish family has seven children, and households with ten or more children are not uncommon.

Yet birth rates alone do not explain the group's rapid growth. Amish babies do not automatically grow into Amish adults. Children born to Amish parents must choose to join the Amish church through the ritual of baptism in their late teens or early twenties. (Those who do not join might affiliate with some other religious tradition or with none at all.) Today 85 percent or more of these children elect baptism and become adult members of the Amish church, and that percentage is notably higher than it was in the mid-1900s. Amish populations are growing because more children than ever are choosing to align themselves with a way of life that is at odds with surrounding society—a phenomenon we will explore in chapter 5.

Population growth has brought new challenges. For example, burgeoning demography puts pressure on Amish farming communities to acquire more land and, eventually, to consider abandoning their plows for nonfarm jobs—jobs that, in turn, raise new questions about what it means to be Amish (chapter 7). Booming populations have also prompted the establishment of new settlements in more states and in far-flung portions of states with existing Amish communities. As a result, today Amish people are rubbing shoulders with neighbors in more and more places, forging new connections and sometimes generating conflict (chapter 8).

Numeric growth has gone hand-in-hand with increasing diversity in Amish lifestyles. As they spread to new areas, Amish families find themselves in a wider range of settings that color their lives—from suburbanizing Delaware and tourist-attracting eastern Ohio to depopulating pockets of upstate New York and remote regions of the Rocky Mountains. In many places today Amish women are more likely to be found behind Walmart or Target shopping carts than around an old-fashioned quilting frame. More men are trading milk cows for small business entrepreneurship or, in some communities, punching a time-clock on a factory floor. Amish buggies in some locations trek nighttime backroads with a single oil-burning lantern hanging to one side, while others travel busy byways with red LED lights and bright orange slow-moving-vehicle triangles, and still others sport a flashing white strobe light on their roof. A summer afternoon picnic may be the most notable diversion some Amish families enjoy, while others winter in Florida or stay in motels on cross-country vacations they arrange with drivers to visit national parks in the West.

One feature of Amish life that fuels diversity is the group's tradition of small-scale community. Amish society has no bureaucracy that can impose complete uniformity. The church has no national or regional conferences, dioceses, or headquarters, no offices, seminaries, or think tanks. Instead, the basic unit of Amish life, beyond the family, is the local church comprised of twelve to eighteen households. Since there are some twenty-two hundred such churches, each with its own

TABLE 1.1: PRACTICES COMMON TO ALL AMISH GROUPS

Rural residence	Lay ministers
German-based dialect	Church-regulated dress
Eighth-grade education	Selective use of technology
Church services in homes	Horse-and-buggy transportation
Small local churches	Nonparticipation in the military

leadership and making its own decisions about technology and other expressions of faith, there are potentially more than twenty-two hundred different ways of being Amish!

Yet there remains a core of common features across the Amish world. The Amish are a Christian church that traces its origins to the Protestant Reformation of the 1500s. Their theological beliefs, as we'll see, are codified in the Bible and in key religious texts that all Amish churches use to instruct their youth in the faith. As well, all Amish use horse and buggy and do not hold driver's licenses. All speak a German dialect as their first language, but they also learn to read, write, and speak English as their second language. None pursue higher education. All wear distinctive clothing—though the particular patterns and colors vary from one group to another—and adult men grow beards. All of these factors make the Amish a distinctive ethno-religious group, but one whose growth, spread, and localized organization militate against complete uniformity.

The Amish and American Society

The Amish may stand apart from the American mainstream in many ways, but their identity is also shaped by how the rest of us imagine and treat them. Government regulation and media representations influence the relationship of insider and outsider and contribute to the formulation of Amish identity.

For example, government decisions to grant minority dissenters certain rights or exemptions necessarily define who is eligible for special treatment and, in turn, affect internal group dynamics. When the U.S. Congress granted the Amish an exemption from participating in Social Security, an exemption based on long-standing Amish opposition to insurance and their documented practice of caring for their elderly, Congress assumed that the Amish were an economically self-sufficient community with few ties to outside employers. So the exemption covered self-employed Amish workers or Amish employees of Amish employers.

The Amish were not as economically isolated as Congress imagined, but the legal exemption had the effect of providing an economic incentive for Amish employees to avoid working for outsiders. Since the Amish church strongly discourages members from collecting Social Security benefits, those who choose to work for outsiders—and are thus not exempt under the law—must pay into a system from which they receive nothing in return, while those who work for a fellow church member are not encumbered with Social Security payroll taxes.

Likewise, when non-Amish drivers provide taxi service to Amish families who won't own cars, the Amish choice to reject driving is made easier and reinforces the Amish sense that not having a driver's license is an essential element of Amish identity—after all, outsiders facilitate the decision to forego car ownership! And when non-Amish advertisers use horse-and-buggy silhouettes to sell products they label "Amish," the wider world reveals its dependence on an Amish identity linked to horses. The cachet of Amish-themed tourism and television shows exists to the degree that Americans perceive the Amish to be different, and that desire for them to remain exotic provides a sort of social space in which the Amish can be acceptably nonconformists—though not always in ways the rest of us think they should be, as the Punxsutawney GPS story suggests.

The countercultural example of the Amish—an example that defies mainstream American ideas about progress, the role of individuals in community, and even the sources of happiness—acts as both a lens and a prism, focusing the cultural assumptions the rest of us hold dear while revealing a spectrum of Amish practices that expand our understanding of their way of life. Understanding the Amish involves taking them seriously on their own terms, even as we recognize that those terms are never entirely their own. In that sense, the Amish story may say something about the broader dynamics of multicultural America.

Finding Our Way

As we begin our journey, familiarity with a few terms and definitions will help us find our way. As mentioned above, the basic religious unit in Amish life is the *church district*, an entity that is somewhat akin to a Protestant congregation or a Catholic parish. The Amish do not have church buildings, however. Instead, members gather for Sunday worship in one another's homes or in a family's barn or shop, rotating meetings from one household to another. Church districts are laid out geographically, with the families living in a particular place—often defined by rural roads, streams, railroad tracks, or other landmarks—constituting the district. As children are born and new families move into the district, the number of people may grow too large to meet comfortably in homes. At that point, the district divides and forms two districts from one. As a result, church districts nationwide are roughly the same size—there are no Amish "mega-churches"—with an average of about 150 people (adults and children) in each.

TABLE 1.2: THE TWELVE LARGEST SETTLEMENTS, 2015

Settlement	State	Number of Church Districts	Estimated Population
Lancaster County Area	Pennsylvania	204	34,070
Holmes County Area	Ohio	257	33,410
Elkhart/LaGrange Area	Indiana	168	23,020
Geauga County Area	Ohio	115	17,020
Adams County Area	Indiana	57	8,270
Nappanee Area	Indiana	42	5,750
Daviess County Area	Indiana	29	4,570
Arthur Area	Illinois	30	4,200
Mifflin County Area	Pennsylvania	28	3,360
Allen County Area	Indiana	21	3,045
Indiana County Area	Pennsylvania	21	2,795
New Wilmington Area	Pennsylvania	19	2,415

Source: http://www2.etown.edu/amishstudies/Largest_Settlements_2015.asp.
Note: The average number of people per district varies by settlement. Holmes County, for example, has 130 per district, while Lancaster County averages 165, yielding a larger population for that settlement.

A cluster of church districts in a particular geographic location is known as a *settlement*. In 2015 there were 500 settlements across thirty-one states and the provinces of Ontario and New Brunswick. Some settlements, such as those in Holmes County, Ohio, or Lancaster County, Pennsylvania, include several hundred districts and thousands of Amish people. Other settlements are quite small and might contain only one or two districts. In neither case—large settlements nor small ones—do the Amish live in isolation. Everywhere they live mixed among rural neighbors of other faiths and traditions. The Amish do not live in exclusive colonies. When non-Amish chambers of commerce use a line like "Visit Amish Country!" to boost regional tourism, they are pointing to a real phenomenon—a concentration of Amish people living in a given place—but there is nothing like an Amish "country" in the sense of a set-aside reservation or bounded space.

Finally, the Amish often refer to those who are not Amish as *the English*. All Amish people are bilingual, but their first language is a German dialect and English is their second language—one that they use especially as they interact with the wider world. As a result, they refer generally to all outsiders with the "English" label. This text will use the terms non-Amish and the English as synonyms.

CHAPTER TWO

Amish Roots

MOST AMISH FAMILIES OWN A THICK BOOK—MORE than a thousand pages in length—entitled *Martyrs Mirror* (or *Martyr Spiegel*, in the German edition). This hefty tome offers an account of church history, beginning with the death of Jesus Christ and continuing through the 1600s. But it's not just any account of religious history. *Martyrs Mirror* focuses on the persecution of religious dissenters, faithful minorities who suffered at the hands of the powerful, and those who were scorned by "the world" as they sought to follow the humble and nonviolent example of Jesus.

Few Amish households read aloud from *Martyrs Mirror* on a regular basis (the language in both the German edition and in the English translation is a bit archaic), but Amish people know the stories and often measure themselves against the example of the martyrs. The stories convey the message that there is suffering in this life, that Christian faithfulness is not popular, and that the world is not to be fully trusted.

Although Amish people in contemporary North America have not been beheaded or burned at the stake like those whose stories appear in the thick martyr book, some Amish in the twentieth and twenty-first centuries have sat in jail or paid stiff fines for refusing to serve in the military, send their children to high school, install smoke detectors in their homes, or place orange slow-moving-vehicle emblems on their buggies. And when they pay a price for going against the grain, they believe they are aligning themselves with their spiritual ancestors.

A Radical Heritage

When the Amish tell their story, they often begin with the Protestant Reformation that shook sixteenth-century Europe. In the early 1500s many things that Europeans had long taken for granted seemed up for grabs. Conquistadors told stories of unknown continents to the west, the printing press circulated new ideas with uncommon speed, inflation destabilized local economies, and vocal critics condemned social institutions as rotten to the core.[1]

The Roman Catholic Church that had long held Western European society together on earth and assured one's journey to heaven also came in for its share of criticism. Figures such as Martin Luther and John Calvin questioned church doctrine and structure and eventually split with Rome, establishing groups that became known as Protestant churches.

At this point, the Amish story focuses on a small group of radical dissenters who questioned the whole premise of the medieval state-church system in which the government mandated correct belief and the church blessed civil and military activity. The dissenters, who gathered in small groups in the Netherlands, Switzerland, and German-speaking central Europe, insisted that a true church would be composed only of those who separated themselves from the corrupting influence of the world and obediently followed the teachings of Jesus, including his commands to live humbly and to reject violence even in self-defense.

The radicals dismissed the long-standing practice of routinely baptizing infants, a practice that made virtually everyone a church member and linked Christianity with citizenship. Instead they proposed that baptism—the Christian rite of initiation into the church—should be a mark of voluntary commitment and therefore fitting only for those who understood the implications of a disciplined life. As a result, these dissenters received the nickname *Anabaptists* (re-baptizers) because they had already been baptized as infants years before the Reformation began and now were advocating baptizing adults. In time, some Anabaptists became known as *Mennonites*, thanks to the notoriety of Menno Simons, an influential Anabaptist leader in the Netherlands.

Anabaptists affirmed the basic theological beliefs that other Christians did. But the Anabaptist conviction that the true church was an alternative community, distinct from larger society and not responsible for morally propping up the political order, sharply distinguished them from both Catholics and mainstream Protestants. Despite the fact that Anabaptists numbered only a few thousand, their presence threatened the established order of religious and civic life. Officials condemned them as subversives and used condemnation, imprisonment, and execution to stem the growth of the community. Between 1527 and 1614 as many as twenty-five hundred Anabaptists were killed—many of their stories fill the last half of the *Martyrs Mirror*— and their deaths served to confirm, for the Anabaptists, the wisdom of renouncing "worldly" society with its brutality and inhumanity.

To this day, stories of these martyr ancestors figure in some of the hymns the Amish sing in their Sunday morning worship. The *Ausbund* hymnal, published as early as 1564, includes songs written by Anabaptists jailed in Passau, Bavaria, and awaiting execution. Other *Ausbund* hymns recount the suffering of the faithful, such as the thirty-two-stanza ballad about Hans Haslibacher, an Anabaptist who was beheaded in 1571.

> Now when he was apprehended,
> Tormented and tortured severely,
> Because of his faith alone,
> Nevertheless he remained steadfast
> In his torture, anguish, and pain, [saying]:
>
> "I am willing and prepared,
> My death certainly brings me great joy,

That I should depart from [here].
But may God be merciful
To those who sentenced me to death."[2]

For the Amish, Hans Haslibacher is a model of faith not simply because he was a martyr, but because he embraced suffering in joy and asked for mercy for his persecutors.

Jakob Ammann and the Birth of the Amish

Persecution—or, more accurately, the waning of persecution—provided the context for the emergence of the Amish as a distinct Anabaptist group. For a century and a half, Anabaptist identity had been nurtured in the fires of opposition. Then, in the later 1600s as Europeans grew weary of wars over religion, the possibility of toleration dawned for once-harried Anabaptists. For those who had long been leery of "the world," how were they to respond when that world now seemed on the brink of accepting them? For some Anabaptists, the advent of toleration was a welcome reprieve for which they had long hoped and prayed. For others, the possibility of social acceptance was a dangerous temptation that needed to be resisted. These differing responses to changing circumstances lay at the heart of Amish origins.[3]

By the mid-1600s Swiss and German Anabaptists had learned to survive by moving to more remote Alpine valleys or by heading north to the Rhine River Valley where they farmed the land of nobles seeking to rebuild estates ruined in the Thirty Years War (1618–1648). These nobles were willing to extend a haven to religious dissenters in exchange for their labor as loyal tenants.

Although Swiss authorities continued to issue edicts against the Anabaptists and kept them from taking up most trades and professions, there is considerable evidence that the Anabaptists' neighbors were coming to admire and befriend them, often shielding them from official harassment and angering state church pastors by saying that the Anabaptists were model Christians. Indeed, in the 1670s and 1680s some of these Swiss admirers converted to the Anabaptist fold, which resulted in much hand-wringing on the part of Protestant officials in the Swiss city-state of Bern. One report from 1680 on such

Village near Erlenbach, Switzerland, where Jakob Ammann was likely born in 1644. He was baptized as an infant into the Reformed Church, converted to Anabaptism by 1680, and about 1693 left Switzerland to move to Alsace. *Credit: Donald B. Kraybill*

converts noted that a tailor named Jakob Ammann from near the village of Erlenbach had become "infected with the Anabaptist sect."[4]

Ammann had been born in 1644. Little information survives about his wife, Verena Stüdler, or their children. Sometime after Ammann converted to Anabaptism he was ordained as a church leader with the authority to baptize others and preside at communion, a Christian ritual sometimes known as the Lord's Supper or eucharist that memorializes the death of Jesus Christ.

Around 1693 the Ammann household left Switzerland and moved north to Alsace, in what is today eastern France, eventually settling near the village of Sainte-Marie-aux-Mines. The Ammanns were not alone. By the early 1690s more than fifty Anabaptist families were living in the area and benefitting from the benign neglect of tolerant lords who overlooked religious dissent.

Pleasant as Alsatian life may have been, the comfortable religious situation made Ammann uneasy. He soon began calling for sharper distinction between Anabaptists and members of "worldly" society, and he criticized fellow Anabaptists who tried to boost their status by making appearances at state-sanctioned churches. Indeed, it seems that by 1693 Ammann had become the most articulate spokesperson for a vigorous Anabaptist renewal movement.[5] Among other things, Ammann called for a more frequent observation of the Lord's Supper, and he insisted that the ritual include a ceremony in which church members literally washed one another's feet, imitating Jesus who had washed his disciples' feet as an act of service and humility.

Most strikingly, Ammann drew on an older Dutch Anabaptist document to teach the practice of shunning those who were excommunicated from the church. The church was not an otherworldly spiritual club, Ammann pointed out, but a group to which one was committed and accountable in practical, everyday ways. Being part of the church had clear social implications and so did leaving the church. Shunning involved the symbolic social avoidance of those who fell into persistent and unrepentant sin. Shunning did not involve breaking off all communication, but church members would not eat at the same table with someone under discipline. Ammann took pains to explain that excommunication and shunning were not to be punishments but rather a warning and a way of helping stumbling members realize the seriousness of their offense against God and, in turn, prompting repentance and restoration.

Ammann's efforts at boosting Anabaptist distinctiveness in Alsace, where a lack of persecution might lull them into complacency, stood in contrast to prevailing sentiments back in Switzerland. There, still-stigmatized Anabaptists were open to finding small ways to get in the good graces of their neighbors. In fact, some Anabaptists in the old Swiss communities regarded Ammann's reforms as abrupt departures from long-standing custom. In reply, Ammann pointed to the Dordrecht Confession, a sixty-year-old Dutch Anabaptist statement that taught both shunning and the footwashing ritual. These were not innovations, Ammann insisted, but practices that stood on clear biblical and Dutch Mennonite precedent. Ammann

and his followers may also have been influenced by Pietism—a renewal movement in German Lutheran and Reformed churches.
During the late 1600s Radical Pietists in the Rhine Valley were also
advocating the practice of shunning and had held up the Dordrecht
Confession as a doctrinal blueprint for those in their circles.[6]

In late summer and fall of 1693, Ammann and several supporters
traveled from Alsace to Switzerland to impress upon Swiss Anabaptists the merits of Ammann's reform agenda. They also chided the
Swiss for being too cozy with "the world." The encounters did not go
well. Letters documenting the debates suggest that Ammann and his
group were aggressive and demanding, while the Swiss Anabaptists,
particularly their senior elder, Hans Reist, were often dismissive and
condescending. At one point, when Reist sent word that he was too
busy with his farm work to be bothered with the Alsatian delegation,
Ammann "almost became enraged and immediately placed Hans
Reist, along with six other ministers, under the ban as a heretic," leaving others at the gathering "horrified" and pleading for reconciliation.[7]

Later, Ammann said he had acted too rashly and asked for Reist's
forgiveness, but Reist rebuffed the gesture, perpetuating a permanent
breach in fellowship between his church and the "Ammann-ish" group
that now existed within the wider Anabaptist community. The two
most contested issues remained the degree of separation from worldly
society and the practice of shunning.

Ammann's faction eventually became known as Amish. Many of
Ammann's Swiss and Palatinate supporters began moving to the
Alsatian valley of Sainte-Marie-aux-Mines, where they coalesced into
a stronger community. Between 1694 and 1696 alone, some sixty households arrived from the Swiss canton of Bern, and by 1699 Amish
families owned many of the valley's farms and were heavily involved
in the local timber and sawmill business. The influx changed the
region's composition and, over time, stirred some local resentment as
the Amish became more numerous.

Longtime residents recognized the new group as "the Jakob
Ammann Party" or "the Jakob Ammann Group."[8] Indeed, records reveal that Ammann often witnessed legal documents and represented
his people to civil authorities. In 1696, for example, he successfully
won for his flock exemption from participating in the militia. In 1701

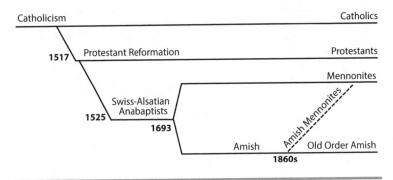

Fig. 2.1. Anabaptist–Amish Timeline, 1517–1900

Ammann represented his people to local officials in a case involving orphaned Amish children. Typically, civil authorities appointed guardians for orphans, but Ammann said his church would take responsibility for its own children. Remarkably, the grand bailiff agreed and ordered the town clerk to permit the Amish to act "according to their customary procedures."[9]

In 1712 the political environment suddenly changed when French King Louis XIV ordered the expulsion of Anabaptists from his domains in Alsace, "with no exceptions . . . [including] even the oldest who have been there for a long time." The Amish community around Sainte-Marie-aux-Mines, which had prospered for two decades was scattered in a matter of months.[10] Families ended up in other parts of southern Germany and the Rhine Valley or in territories neighboring royal Alsace. In most cases officials in these new places barred the Amish from buying land, so families became managers or leaseholders on estates owned by absentee landlords.[11]

Two Waves of Immigration

Despite their desire for separation from "the world," the Amish were much like their neighbors in at least one respect. In the early 1700s up and down the Rhine Valley the prospect of immigration to North America was alluring. Amish emigrants were a small part of a larger movement of German-speaking people who crossed the Atlantic in the first part of the 1700s and again in the early 1800s.

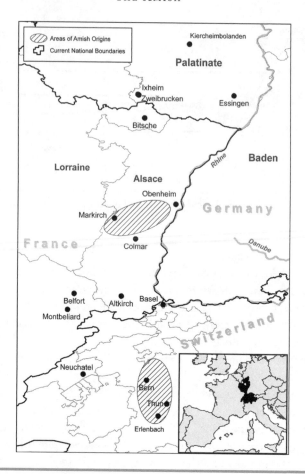

Fig. 2.2. Areas of Amish Origin in Europe ca. 1700 *Map prepared by St. Lawrence University Libraries GIS Program*

Between 1736 and 1770 about five hundred Amish arrived through the port of Philadelphia and settled in southeastern Pennsylvania. Although the first Amish families made their homes in Berks County, by the time of the American Revolution they had begun concentrating in Lancaster County. In the decades that followed, descendants of these eighteenth-century immigrants formed new settlements in central and western Pennsylvania, and on into the Midwest.[12]

Between 1815 and 1860 a second wave of some three thousand Amish immigrants came to North America. These newcomers were seeking both economic opportunity and freedom from compulsory military service, which was becoming more common in Europe. Few of these nineteenth-century Amish arrivals settled in Pennsylvania, choosing instead to move directly to the Great Lakes states and to Ontario.

Emigration from Europe weakened the Amish church there, and in the late 1800s the Amish presence in Europe faded. The departure of many young adults for North America undercut the group's vitality. As membership declined, pressure grew to intermarry with members of more respectable state churches. In 1937 the last European Amish congregation, a small church in the Palatinate village of Ixheim, merged with a nearby Mennonite group.

The Amish story in Europe had come to a close, but it was thriving, under different circumstances, in the midst of modernizing North America. There, by the mid-1800s, Amish immigrants and their descendants had established more than two dozen settlements from Pennsylvania to Iowa. Among those that persist to this day are ones in Lancaster (since the 1760s) and Mifflin (1791) Counties, Pennsylvania; Holmes County, Ohio (1803); LaGrange County, Indiana (1841); Kalona, Iowa (1846); and Arthur, Illinois (1865).

Defining the "Old Order"

Even as the Amish put down roots, the young United States they now called home was rapidly transforming socially, economically, and politically. A competitive and open market with an accent on individual consumption was shaking up long-assumed social habits. Free from the constraints of "old world" social class and able to accumulate property that would have been unthinkable in Europe, thanks to the removal of Native people, white Americans enjoyed remarkable social mobility. Yeomen farmers could acquire the trappings of genteel society, and many worked long and hard to give the appearance of not having to work at all. Families transformed their homes from centers of production into places of retreat, turning a work space that might have once housed the family loom or cobbler's tools into a parlor, complete with stuffed furniture and display objects whose only purpose was "for show."[13]

In 1862, as Amish bishop David Beiler looked around his Lancaster County, Pennsylvania, neighborhood, the results of this shift were all too clear. Beiler was certain that "whoever has not experienced" the "great changes during these [past] sixty years . . . can scarcely believe it." In his youth "there was no talk of fine shoes and boots nor did one know anything of light pleasure vehicles." Homes did not boast sofas, writing desks, carpets, and decorative dishes, as was now the fashion. "It was customary to hear the spinning wheel hum or sing in almost every farmhouse," Beiler recalled. Now, "the domestic cotton goods which are to be had at such low price, have almost displaced the home-made materials" and young people hire themselves out for wages so they can buy the latest horse harness or "strange colored fine store clothes."[14]

Beiler had a keen eye for social and economic change and for the cultural implications of such change. Life in the young United States had offered religious liberty to harried Anabaptists, but it also promised to replace the wisdom of local tradition with a consumer culture of personal fulfillment and the adoption of patriotic causes. Indeed, America's Protestant churches, for the most part, blessed the refinement and good taste that marked emerging middle-class mores. Moreover, religious revivalism and denominational organization seemed to cast *church* in terms of either individual experience or a set of programs and budgets, rather than local relationships and ethical discipline.

Amish leaders struggled to know how to navigate these cultural currents. Notes from meetings of Amish ministers in the 1840s in Holmes County, Ohio, reveal that leaders in that place repeatedly stressed the importance of simplicity in personal appearance and a skepticism toward new consumer goods, but the frequency with which they admonished their flock suggest the sort of countervailing pressures they faced.[15]

Beginning in 1862 Amish church leaders from Pennsylvania to Iowa gathered annually to discuss common concerns. The American Civil War, then raging, was fairly easy for them to address. They reaffirmed Anabaptist pacifism and in most cases, it seems, young men heeded the church's teaching. How to respond to other forces reshaping their communities was less clear. A majority of Amish leaders seemed ready to embrace a change-minded agenda, to the chagrin of those who wished to stand by the "old order" of simplicity, small-scale community, and tradition-guided church life that resisted being pressed into a popular Protestant mold.

In the end, about two-thirds of Amish churches in the 1860s opted for a more fluid and change-minded identity. These churches stopped gathering for worship in members' homes, as their ancestors had long done, and constructed church buildings. They replaced the authoritative memory of the aged with written constitutions that could be amended by majority votes, and adopted the style and programming of their Protestant neighbors.

By the early 1900s these change-minded Amish churches had aligned themselves with their more progressive Anabaptist cousins, the Mennonites, thereafter morphing into Mennonite congregations and formally joining one Mennonite group or another.[16] In other cases, progressive Amish families simply assimilated into mainstream society and discarded religious particularity entirely. Such was the case, for example, of seismologist Charles Richter, who developed the Richter Scale of earthquake magnitude. Although he had deep roots in the Amish community of Butler County, Ohio, where he was born, his autobiography suggests his family had passed on to him virtually nothing of his Amish heritage.[17]

In contrast, the tradition-minded or *Old Order* Amish of the 1860s formed the nucleus of what would become the Amish church that remains distinguishable in the twenty-first century. These Amish rejected the programmatic approach to church that they saw in Sunday schools, mission budgets, and seminary education. Instead, they focused all the more on the collective discipline of the local church and traditional interpretations of Scripture.

In broad strokes, the old order tradition that took shape in the mid-1800s was a cluster of commitments that continue to shape the contours of Amish life today:

- plainness, simplicity, and a rejection of consumer culture, combined with an expectation that the church can and should collectively prescribe such things as clothing and home furnishings.

- church defined in small-scale, local terms, resulting in a rejection of church buildings, denominational structures, and salaried clergy.
- a clear sense that tradition is a trustworthy guide for navigating an uncertain future and for maintaining social balance, matched with skepticism toward progressive forms of authority such as science, popular opinion, or professional expertise.

Navigating the Modern World

It should be clear by now that the Old Order Amish did not forge their identity around rejecting cars or telephones. In the 1860s those pieces of technology did not exist! But old order dispositions pointed the direction in which Amish choices about consumer technology would unfold in the decades to come. For example, after 1910, the Amish rejected automobile ownership in favor of continued horse and buggy transportation. Cars quickly became status symbols, while the more egalitarian buggy slowed the pace of life and kept family and community life local and face-to-face.

Constructing and reconstructing the boundaries of Amish life was a dynamic process that involved forces both inside and outside Amish society. The rise of the welfare state, for example, challenged the Amish notion that the church alone would provide for members' needs when family finances proved inadequate. Resisting public (and commercial) insurance programs, Amish people rejected Social Security when it was extended to self-employed farmers in 1955. After prolonged conflict with federal tax collectors, the Amish received congressional exemption from the program, and from Medicare, in 1965. Today self-employed Amish people and Amish employees of Amish employers are exempt from these taxes and also barred from receiving benefits. Apart from these exceptions, Amish individuals pay all other income, property, inheritance, and sales taxes just as any other U.S. resident would.[18]

The Amish principle of nonresistant pacifism also set them at odds with the state. During the First World War a number of Amish men were imprisoned and abused because of their refusal to fight and, no doubt, because they spoke a German dialect which marked them as political pariahs during the nation's war with Germany.

Going to church on a winter Sunday morning near Jamesport, Missouri.
Credit: Don Burke

Beginning in the 1940s draft boards were more understanding of Amish pacifism, granted them conscientious objector status, and often assigned them to work in civilian hospitals—a pattern that held throughout the years of Cold War conscription. Still, not all Amish families were comfortable with the state sending their young men off to urban places of employment. Between 1953 and 1973 a half dozen new Amish settlements sprouted in Ontario, comprised of households emigrating from the United States and disenchanted with what they felt was overly intrusive U.S. government.

The vast majority of Amish remained in the United States, however, and over the course of the twentieth century their numbers rose substantially. In 1970 there were some 50,000 Amish (adult church members and unbaptized children combined). By 2000 there were 180,000 and in 2015 there were 300,000. The old order is alive and well in contemporary North America even as its members have charted a distinctive path in the midst of modernity.

CHAPTER THREE

Living the Old Order

IN 1953 CHARLES WILSON, THE CEO OF GENERAL MO-
tors, told members of Congress that "what was good for the
country was good for General Motors and vice versa."[1] Although Wilson had a reputation for exaggeration, in this
case he had articulated a deeply held American assumption
that the values epitomized by the automobile—personal choice,
sleek modernity, and the undisputed ability of science and engineering to improve life—were aligned with fundamental
American values. Unconstrained by the collective schedules of
trains and trolleys, cars expressed the country's individualistic
impulse. Automakers wielded the authority of technology and
mass production to combine innovation, consumer appeal,
and planned obsolescence in a product that came to represent
America itself.

The Amish have been much more skeptical of the values
embodied in contemporary car culture, even as they sometimes hire drivers and selectively use motor vehicles for

certain trips. They might well agree that the car exemplifies basic American values, but they are not sure they want those values animating their lives.

The Amish story is much more than simply a narrative of rejecting car ownership, of course. As we've seen, their church communities began to distinguish themselves from the cultural mainstream in the mid-1800s, before the advent of the automobile. Yet the Amish unease with the automobile and their choice to forego personal car ownership says a great deal about how Amish life has diverged from the national norm and taken an old order path. Before we look at the Amish road map, however, we consider the modern American world they see around them.

Life in Modern America

Scholars have long debated the definition of modernity, yet most see a cluster of emphases and activities as central to what it means to be modern. Rationality and efficiency are esteemed, and science and technology—to the degree that they promise greater efficiency through rational processes—are often unquestioned authorities. Being able to do something faster or to increase the quantity of something are self-evident goods that need no justification. No one has to convince us that quicker download speeds are better than slower ones, for example, or sell us on the benefits of more iPhone memory. A recent advertisement for an unlimited phone data plan captured these sentiments with its pitch line: "I need to upload all of it. I need—no, I have the *right* to be unlimited!"[2]

One byproduct of the modern drive for efficiency is that life has become segmented, broken down into separate parts. Work was separated from leisure, residential space was divided from commercial space, and the elderly were segregated into age-defined retirement homes. Media splintered and specialized audiences. Assembly lines were the epitome of modern manufacturing, taking a process and dividing it into discrete stages that were then repeated with maximum efficiency. Consolidated school systems that brought together large numbers of children and then separated them by age and ability were the assembly line's educational parallel, and retail franchise networks played a similar role in the commercial realm.

The emergence of the Internet, smart phones, and wireless technology has promised to blur some of modernity's tidy categories. People can now work from home, shop at work, and perpetually "connect" with others, even on vacation. Nevertheless, this most recent iteration of what some theorists call "late modernity" or "liquid modernity" continues to share a firm commitment to the basic outlines of rational efficiency. Mobile apps, for example, have become ubiquitous because they promise specialized, on-demand, Internet shortcuts that seem instantaneous. Moreover, the basic division of time from place that flourishes in a worldwide web of virtual communities, avatars, and anonymity is yet another dimension of modernity's penchant for segmentation.[3]

Alongside these aspects of modernity, United States culture adds its own distinctive stamp. Like other nations, the United States is a country of national myths. There is, for example, the myth of the "melting pot," by which many Americans believe that assimilation of cultural groups is inevitable or benign or both. Perhaps more important has been the myth of individual transcendence, a promise that people can leave all tradition behind and start over anew, that the future is better than the past and that *new* equals *improved*. Americans are much more apt to deal with discontent by leaving a product, group, or situation behind and starting over again rather than sticking with something old and working to improve or adapt it. The rhetoric of individual choice and personal self-improvement has often tied the characteristics of modernity and U.S. culture together into a seamless understanding of the American way of life.

Certainly the principles that characterize modernity have increased material production and raised living standards for many people. They have also come at something of a cost. People primed for efficiency are apt to feel like they are—or should be—in a hurry. Endless choices leave individuals perpetually dissatisfied and lonely, while the segmentation of life, mixed with the powerful allure of technology, can make it seem not only easier, but even *better*, to quickly scan Facebook updates instead of spending time talking with a friend. Although some observers wonder how the Amish can so easily accept the dictates of their tradition, the Amish might ask if contemporary Americans have not thoughtlessly accepted the logic of modernity and national myths. Indeed, in rejecting the broad contours of American life, the Amish may be better able to recognize those contours than highly educated people who swim in the sea of modernity.

In any case, the Amish do not generally share the modern assumptions and American values that animate most aspects of contemporary society. In the next chapter we'll see how the compact and integrated nature of Amish community life diverges from the modern penchant for efficiency of scale and segmentation. For now, we'll consider how Amish religious values and cultural habits emphasize slowing down, placing the community ahead of the individual, and otherwise standing against the cult of the transcendent individual.

Yielding and Following

The Amish teach much that would be familiar in any branch of the Christian tradition—the Trinity, the death and resurrection of Christ, the future reality of heaven and hell, and so on. They believe that the Bible is the word of God, they practice rituals of baptism and communion, and strongly encourage daily devotions.

But the Amish tradition is also a specific expression of Christianity with distinctive emphases. For example, the Amish dissent from displays of national patriotism, which they see as a form of idolatry. Compared with many other churches, the Amish place a heavy emphasis on following the example of Jesus in everyday life. Scripture reading in Amish worship centers on the stories of Jesus and his teaching as found in the four Gospels of the New Testament. What the Amish see in these texts is a picture of humility, obedience, and nonresistant love. Jesus was obedient to God the Father and submitted to painful crucifixion as an expression of his compassion for humanity.

A German term that pulls together many of these values is *Gelassenheit* (yieldedness, yielding to others), and it is a central expression of the Amish way.[4] "Gelassenheit means more than outward obedience," an Ohio Amish deacon explains. "It is also the inward attitude to this obedience. It is the way that God's work on earth was completed. Christ revealed this way through his life."[5] The examples of the Anabaptist martyrs who died without fighting back echo

Children absorb the Amish way of humility, simplicity, and obedience at a young age. *Credit: Don Burke*

through Amish history and remind Amish people that following Jesus is a real, if costly and dangerous, possibility.

Amish spirituality stresses self-surrender. Yielding to God, to the church, and to others is part and parcel of being Amish. "Thy will be done," a line from the Lord's Prayer—a prayer that is frequently on Amish lips—epitomizes their confidence in divine providence and a spirit of humble acceptance. The Amish are not fatalists and do not believe in predestination, but they do have a remarkably strong sense of giving up self.

In 2006 after a non-Amish gunman invaded an Amish school in Nickel Mines, Pennsylvania, and shot ten young girls, five of them fatally, Amish family members and neighbors responded with remarkable words and acts of forgiveness. Some observers wondered how the Amish could express forgiveness so readily in such circumstances and characterized the Amish response as unnatural. In fact, forgiveness was not easy for those caught up in the Nickel Mines tragedy. But although forgiveness was difficult, it did not strike the Amish as an unnatural act. Forgiveness involves some element of giving up—giving up bitterness, giving up revenge—and Amish life is saturated with routines and rituals of giving up—giving up personal choices about dress, technology, and higher education. For Amish people, forgiveness is not easy, but it fits into a larger pattern of self-surrender that marks their life. In contrast, most Americans are trained—even in their religious lives—not to sacrifice anything and to have it all. That sort of orientation is worlds apart from an Amish approach to faith.

Everyday Faith

Amish spirituality is neither highly emotional nor given to articulate reflection, but it is pervasive and public. It is not a private or a Sunday-only affair. It permeates everyday life in a myriad of ways. "Plain dress is sometimes understood as only [an effort] to be different," an Amish writer has said, "but it is much more." Those in mainstream society "wear their clothes to enhance their reputation or to show off their bodies or to demonstrate their wealth. This is an expression of self-will." Individuals could be left to make clothing choices all on their own, "but we insist on a uniformity of dress decided by the church for two reasons." First, "because self-will must be yielded" and, second, because "it takes away competitiveness" and "provides an escape from the fashions of this world."[6] Prohibitions on jewelry, including wrist watches and wedding rings, diminish individual adornment and illustrate one's submission to the pattern of the church.

Plainness also permeates home décor and is evident in personal interactions. Averting eye contact or pausing before responding to a question are expressions of Gelassenheit that stand in contrast to an assertive, boisterous personality. An emphasis on humility prizes small-scale, face-to-face relationships over big institutions, grand

Plain dress distinguishes the Amish from their neighbors watching a summer parade in the town of Arthur, Illinois. *Credit: Don Burke*

buildings, and sprawling organizations. Amish churches meet for worship in the homes of members, and that pattern keeps congregations small and local. A handful of families comprise a local church district that is defined geographically. Households do not "shop around" for an Amish church they prefer, but participate in the district in which they live.

Horse and buggy transportation expresses and reinforces Amish values. As one publication aimed at church members explains, the unlimited access to automobiles in wider society has resulted in people "heading off in all directions and leading essentially separate lives. . . . Members of the same [non-Amish] church may live ten, twenty, or even fifty miles apart, attending church [on Sunday mornings] and yet be totally unattached to the life of the community."[7] The Amish do not view cars as evil but as tools that can easily foster the problematic human impulse to put one's own desires and priorities first. Prohibiting car ownership but allowing members to hire non-Amish drivers for some trips is not, from the Amish point of view, hypocritical. It is, rather, a deeply consistent expression of their values. In both cases what the church is striving to discourage is individual autonomy. Hiring a driver places one in the debt of another person, promotes cooperation, limits frivolous trips, and ensures that no one travels too far alone.

Similarly, the old order critique of public education during the mid-1900s focused on the size and scale of consolidated schools that encouraged competitive achievement, critical thinking, and specialization. Amish schools, in contrast, operate on a small scale, stop with eighth grade, and promote values of cooperation, submission, and humility.

This spirituality of submission may strike modern onlookers as crushing. What about free self-expression, self-determination, and making the most of your life on your own terms? Amish life does, in fact, allow for some creative outlets. From uniquely tended flower beds to multicolored quilt tops to craftsmen who find new ways to refit electrical machinery so it can be run with church-approved power sources, ingenuity is no stranger to the Amish home and shop. Furthermore, individual personality traits and preferences texture Amish life in ways that cannot be communicated in postcard images. Nevertheless, it is true that Amish life does not offer the flexibility and freedom that many Americans have come to assume as a self-evident good. To be Amish is to make a choice to surrender many choices to the wisdom of the group and to submit to tradition, to the conviction of older generations, and to church leaders.

Ordnung—A Moral Road Map

Although the tradition-minded Amish of the 1800s rejected the path of eager adaptation and assimilation to mainstream American ways, they did not try to freeze their customs or stop all change. If they had, there would not today be thousands of Amish buggies made of fiberglass or hundreds of old order households experimenting with solar power. What the Amish have done is regulate the pace and direction of change by deferring to the wisdom of the group and of tradition rather than to the impulse of individual preference or the direction of marketing mavens.

The Amish navigate the future using a moral road map they call *Ordnung*. A German term that literally means "order," Ordnung sets the boundaries of what they see as a divinely ordered life. It is the collected wisdom of past generations addressed to a host of everyday situations. As a Christian church, the Amish regard the Bible as their ultimate authority in moral matters, but Ordnung offers guidance for the many topics on which Scripture is silent by applying biblical principles to contemporary life. Ordnung prescribes and proscribes, both directing and limiting what a person does. Ordnung dictates a particular style of clothing and how one should travel to work. It mandates certain activities on Sunday and labels others taboo. In general, Ordnung governing religious rituals—such as the order of worship on a Sunday morning—is more resistant to change than Ordnung surrounding what technology is permissible in an Amish-owned retail store. But all aspects of life, to some degree, fall under this sacred canopy.

TABLE 3.1: CHURCH ORDNUNG VERSUS HOUSEHOLD DISCRETION

Examples of Things Governed by Church Ordnung
Styles and dimension of clothing, hats, and bonnets
Color and style of buggy
Format and sequence of elements in church service
Types of technology used in the home
Marriage within the church
Prohibition on filing lawsuits

Examples of Things Generally Left to Household Discretion
Food and diet preferences
Subscribing to a local newspaper
Choice of occupation (farming, shop, carpentry, etc.)
Medical care (frequency, type)
How often to hire a non-Amish driver
Whether and where to buy property

"A respected Ordnung," one minister has written, "generates peace, love, contentment, equality, and unity." From the outside, deference to tradition might seem "impractical" or "an outdated thing," he acknowledged. Other Christians may even denounce it as cold legalism. But, this minister contended, individualism can also be a cruel master, and as Madison Avenue dictates fads and fashions, individual choice turns out to be an illusion. Everyone submits to some authority, he argued, and the person who lives by "a time-proven" Ordnung "actually has more freedom . . . than those who are bound to the outside [world]."[8]

Unlike Jewish Mishnah or Islamic Hadith, Amish Ordnung is not written down or studied by Amish scholars. Ordnung is a dynamic oral tradition and it is absorbed more than dictated.[9] Rather than a rule book to be memorized, it is understood to be a way of going about life. Amish people are hard-pressed to enumerate the implicit and explicit elements of Ordnung—"It's just how we do things. It's understood," is their common response when asked to explain the Ordnung—but they know that it is a real presence in everyday life. Ordnung is passed on by parents through the way they raise their children, and fidelity to the Ordnung is formally reaffirmed (or modified) in every local church district twice a year, as we will see in chapter 4.

Ordnung regulates Amish life, but Ordnung flexes or tightens in response to real world developments and the changing social and political contexts in which the Amish find themselves. Church leaders—the bishops, ministers, and deacons—do not create the Ordnung. They see themselves as stewards of a tradition who have a responsibility to make sure that the burden of proof is on any argument for change. Indeed, ordained men and their families must model faithful adherence to the Ordnung and they must uphold somewhat higher standards than others in the church. Bishops have less leeway in pushing the boundaries of acceptable recreation, for example, and their clothing styles are often slightly more severe.

In contrast, ordinary lay members may have a bit more flexibility. Young married couples without children have the greatest flexibility because they are not yet responsible for training the next generation. In some settlements, for example, they might enjoy a Saturday water skiing excursion that would be off-limits for parents with children and

Amish playing shuffleboard in Pinecraft, Florida, a winter haven for Amish retirees. A more relaxed Ordnung prevails here. *Credit: Kimberly Button*

unthinkable for a bishop and his family. As one advances in age and status, the Ordnung becomes more restrictive. At the same time, the Ordnung may be interpreted more loosely to accommodate the special needs of the elderly or those with disabilities. A motorized wheelchair might be acceptable for a man with muscular dystrophy, but his brother who does not have that condition would be prohibited from purchasing a riding lawn mower. Older adults who spend winter months in Pinecraft, Florida, a village on the outskirts of Sarasota that has become a haven for Amish "snow birds," also enjoy a much more flexible Ordnung. In that setting, the use of some electric appliances or air conditioning does not directly challenge the authority of the Ordnung back home, and when retirees return north in March they immediately revert to living within the bounds of the prevailing Ordnung there.

Diversity and Affiliation

In fact, it is precisely because old order values prize local tradition and resist homogenizing pressures from afar that the details of Amish life have never been uniform across the continent. In that sense, Ordnung expresses and validates the particular. For example, Ordnung in Lancaster, Pennsylvania, dictates that buggy tops are gray in color, while the long-standing custom in Ohio is black. The particular patterns of a man's hat or a woman's bonnet also vary from region to region, reflecting different Ordnung traditions in each place. The history of the particular community and the temperament of local church leaders determine a great deal how the Ordnung is understood, interpreted, and enforced. Some churches might resist approving certain changes because they wish to differentiate themselves from a neighboring Amish church that they perceive to be too liberal—or vice versa. In some Amish settlements all the congregations seek to maintain a common Ordnung, while in other places the Ordnung can vary significantly from one church district to the next just a few miles down the road.

Differences in Ordnung have given rise to distinct Amish subgroups, sometimes known as affiliations. Affiliations are loose associations of Amish church districts that share a similar Ordnung. There are some forty different identifiable affiliations. Members of an affiliation may encourage or expect their children to find spouses from within the affiliation, and bishops and ministers may be asked to preach or otherwise participate in the worship service of districts beyond their home but within their affiliation. Lines of affiliation are not rigid and evolve as districts make—or refuse to make—changes in their Ordnung. Affiliations may include more than a hundred church districts or may be comprised of a mere handful. They are not bureaucratic organizations with formal meetings, membership, or affiliationwide leaders. Instead, they are informal networks of Amish churches that recognize one another's Ordnung as similar—or similar enough—to merit closer cooperation than they might afford some other Amish churches. By dint of tradition, an affiliation might be known by a label, such as the Andy Weaver Amish or the Byler Amish, while others have geographically linked monikers, such as the

Ordnung governing technology is more permissive in New Order Amish circles. Farmers might use tractors to bring crops in from the field or even drive to town with a tractor instead of with a horse and buggy. *Credit: Don Burke*

Lancaster Amish, a group that includes districts in the large Lancaster, Pennsylvania, settlement as well as churches with roots in Lancaster but now scattered across seven other states.

Two affiliations on either end of a spectrum suggest the diversity within today's Amish world. The so-called Swartzentruber Amish represent perhaps the most conservative slice of the Amish pie. Tracing their identity to a debate over church discipline in 1917 in Wayne County, Ohio, the Swartzentrubers now have settlements in more than a dozen states. They uphold the most traditional ways of life and their Ordnung is perhaps the most resistant to change. In contrast, the so-called New Order Amish coalesced as an affiliation in 1966, first in Holmes County, Ohio, with a nod to some progressive impulses. The New Order group retains horse and buggy transportation, but lifted some restrictions on household technology, such as in-home landline telephones, and they flavor their religious life with some of the language of evangelical Protestantism. From the

New Order perspective, what sets their group apart are things like strict prohibition against smoking or making sure that parents closely monitor weekend youth activities. But to some other Amish, a relaxed attitude on technology and dress distinguishes the New Order.[10]

Across the spectrum of affiliations, the values of Gelassenheit and the discipline of living within the Ordnung send messages to insider and outsider alike. For those outside the Amish orbit, plainness indicates Amish-ness; for those inside, the degree of plainness signals affiliation. But regardless of affiliation, the very presence of a collective Ordnung to which individuals submit distinguishes the Amish in fundamental ways from their American neighbors. Plainness is not just an ethnic aesthetic but an expression of a deeply seated orientation to the world that runs counter to the values and national myths that animate most American lives. Although being old order is not always the same thing as being old fashioned, the Amish have great respect for tradition and for the wisdom of the past, and in the United States that sets them at odds with a dominant culture in which individual choice, technological know-how, and popular opinion are the reigning and often unquestioned authorities.

Distinctive Amish values also shape formal structures of church and community, as we will see in the next chapter.

CHAPTER FOUR

Community and Church

SIXTY YEARS LATER, THE MEMORY OF HIS AMISH BAP-
tism remained crystal clear for Harvey Yoder. "I'll never
forget kneeling at the front of the congregation and having
our good Bishop Simon Yoder cup water in his hands from a
bowl and gently pour this sacramental sign of cleansing and
commissioning on my head—*im Namen des Vaters und des
Sohnes und des heiligen Geistes* [In the name of the Father and
of the Son and of the Holy Spirit]—and then taking me by
the hand and having me stand as a new born and newly wel-
comed adult member of God's family." Adolescent life could
be complicated, but Yoder's experience of church had left
him confident "that God did indeed love and forgive me."

Yoder's family later left the Amish church. His parents
wanted a religious community that valued verbal evangelism
and missionary work. Leaving also meant that the Yoder
family could drive a car and "we could have telephones instead of going to our [non-Amish] neighbors when we had

to make a call," he remembered. Eventually, Yoder ended up in a Mennonite Church, pursued higher education, and became a licensed counselor and family therapist. Still, six decades later he recognized that "a part of me will always be Amish, the part aiming to live a frugal and unpretentious lifestyle, maintaining strong family commitments, valuing close ties with others in caring communities, as well as about keeping church simple and more about relationships than about expensive real estate and salaried staff."[1]

Not everyone who leaves the Amish community has such warm memories of their upbringing, and the vast majority of those who are baptized never leave. Still, Yoder's memories and reflections illustrate how church and community form individuals through particular practices and institutions. The values of Gelassenheit and the guidance of Ordnung take practical form in the small-scale structures of community and the rituals of the church.

Bigness Ruins Everything

Outsiders might not be surprised that Harvey Yoder's parents left the church, since many onlookers wonder if the commitment necessary to be a member of the Amish community is worth the personal cost.

Yet, Amish people might similarly question the trade-offs that many mainstream folks make without a second thought. Modern-minded people generally believe that the efficiencies gained through economies of scale are more valuable than the close connections and relationships that melt away as institutions mushroom and bureaucracy grows. The Amish are much less ready to make that swap.

"Bigness ruins everything," an Amish man stated categorically. His sentiment is borne out in all sorts of ways across Amish society. Church districts are comprised of no more people than can fit in a private home. Schools are one- or two-room buildings. Few Amish-owned businesses have more than a dozen employees, and those that get much larger often face church pressure to divide or downsize.

The bureaucracy that does exist in Amish society is remarkably limited in size and scope. The church's approach to insurance provides a striking example. The Amish believe that church members bear a divine responsibility to care for one another in times of crisis, such as the aftermath of a house fire or the need to pay a major medical bill.

As a result, they do not purchase commercial insurance nor do they participate in public plans such as Medicare. Instead, they rely on church-centered mutual aid programs to assist families with property losses, health care costs, or even small business product liability. The precise way these mutual aid plans work, and the ways they draw on the financial resources of a wide circle of districts, varies from one community or affiliation to another. But none of the systems involve paid staff, formal office space, or overhead expenses. Volunteer boards and treasurers, working from a kitchen desk, efficiently maintain records, collect money, mail payments, and keep members informed of financial needs.

Other modest institutions include Amish historical libraries and informal trade groups. Libraries typically begin with the hobby interest of a book collector or genealogist who shares a personal collection with those in the community. Other historically minded individuals may donate or combine their books and a dedicated but unprofessional group of library directors will begin meeting and arrange a schedule during which they take turns volunteering to help people who wish to use the materials. Publicity is minimal and budgets are low.

Amish shop owners—cabinet makers, for example, or leather workers—have formed trade groups, but their structure diverges sharply from that of their modern trade group counterparts. Annual gatherings of Amish artisans may attract attendees from settlements across the country. But the gatherings are held at a shop or farm, not in a hotel or downtown convention center. Amish and non-Amish sales people display their wares and network with one another, but the emphasis is not on competition—which, for the Amish, is a vice paired with pride—but on cooperation. Ideas, new products, and even potential markets are shared with a freedom that would astound many English business people. Usually known as "reunions," these trade gatherings attract entire families and not simply Amish men. In fact, the idea of a gathering just for business does not make much sense in Amish circles, both because family businesses generally involve the whole household and also because the separation of work and leisure, so central to modern conceptions of time and life, is foreign to the Amish. The gatherings are recreational events for children and the meals and heavy accent on visiting do turn the events into reunions as much as business opportunities.

The small scale of Amish organizations, from the church district to the mutual aid society, creates a relatively flat and accessible set of relationships. Despite the real power and authority that church leaders hold, Amish society is arguably less hierarchical than modern bureaucracies whose organizational flow charts often illustrate the inaccessibility of top layers of control to those on the bottom rungs.

Relationships in Community

Unlike the efficient bureaucracy of modern life, which sharply separates functions and creates specialized roles, Amish society is a network of dense and overlapping relationships. Amish society is sometimes called a *high-context* culture: one in which people know and relate to one another in multiple ways. In *low-context* modernity, people interact with one another in narrowly defined ways. In this situation a patient is concerned with his dentist's professional qualifications, for example, not the dentist's status as a member of a church or her role in an extended family. For the high-context Amish, in contrast, the school teacher is likely also a relative, and fellow church members are coworkers, and all of those overlapping relationships matter in routine interaction. A person's status is not easily defined as just a deacon or just a shop owner or just a father since a person is seen as functioning in all those ways at once.

In practical terms, this means that Amish community interactions can leave much unsaid because people know a great deal about one another. At the same time, conversation in high-context cultures can easily offend modern sensibilities by crossing the sorts of boundaries that modernity erects to keep life segmented. Thus, what would be considered gossip in a modern, low-context culture is standard information in a high-context setting.

High-context information is central to two Amish correspondence newspapers, *The Budget* and *Die Botschaft*, which extend community beyond face-to-face interactions, but do so in a way that follows the contours of Amish culture.[2] Amish correspondence papers are unique

Conversation is a central feature of high-context culture, and a favorite pastime in Amish circles. *Credit: Don Burke*

in today's world of print journalism. For one thing, both have solid and stable subscription bases that are not being undercut by the Internet or other digital media. Neither paper has headlines, photos, sports pages, comics, or even feature articles. Instead, each week they offer up hundreds of letters, printed in identical columns, from readers across the country. Writers, known as scribes, describe the weather, report on who visited whom in their rural neighborhood, and announce births, injuries, and deaths. All of the letters are in English and most of the writers are women.

The papers are ubiquitous in Amish homes, and this old-fashioned medium seems miles removed from the world of Twitter and YouTube. Yet there are some intriguing parallels. Like Internet interest groups, *The Budget* and *Die Botschaft* bring together people who share mutual interests and whose conversations are grounded in a common discourse of insider knowledge and acceptable topics. The daily routines described in the letters assume horse-and-buggy travel, for example, and virtually every letter mentions which family hosted church services. In that sense, the newspapers are significantly different from online virtual communities, since the life reflected in these pages is absolutely grounded in real-time, face-to-face interactions of Amish church members.

Religious Rhythms

The Amish way is rooted in the religious rhythms that mark Amish church life.[3] Each church district gathers for worship every other Sunday morning. On the intervening Sundays families remain quietly at home with family devotions around the kitchen table or attend a neighboring Amish district that is having church that week.

A worship service lasts for about three hours and is soaked with rituals that express the Christian values Amish hold dear. Adult members and unbaptized children attend worship together, but they group themselves in age and gender cohorts, sitting, in effect, as the family of God rather than as nuclear families. Worship opens with the slow cadence of sixteenth-century hymns whose tunes have been passed on orally for generations. Singing a four-stanza hymn can take fifteen or twenty minutes. The hymns are sung a cappella and in unison. No part of the worship service is rushed.

One of the ministers or the deacon reads aloud one or two chapters from the New Testament. There are long prayers during which everyone kneels in humility before God. And there are two sermons, an initial sermon that may last up to a half hour and a main sermon that takes an hour or more. All this time the congregation has been sitting on backless benches (pregnant women and the elderly may be offered folding chairs for comfort). Ministers stand to preach but do so in the midst of the congregation. As one church publication explains, having everyone on the same floor level "gives the ministry and laity a sense of being on equal grounds."[4] A preachers deliver sermons without prepared texts or even notes—props that suggest he has honed his homiletic skills—but relies on the Holy Spirit to provide the words. Sermons convey a somber and serious tone. There are practical illustrations from nature and daily life, but no jokes and certainly no eye-catching PowerPoint slides or video clips to grab listeners' attention.

Indeed, the entire atmosphere of worship is minimalistic compared with many other places of worship. Worshippers are assembled in the first floor of a home or in the basement or in a shop or

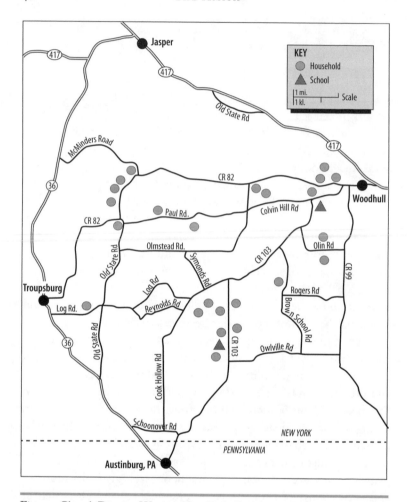

Fig. 4.1. Church District, Western New York. Families within a church district, such as this one, take turns hosting Sunday worship, rotating the meeting place from home to home throughout the year.

barn. Furniture or equipment has been rearranged or moved out, and the district's benches have been moved in, transported from house to house in a special wagon that is the only property the church collectively owns. But there is no pulpit, no candles, stained glass windows, icons, choir, organ, incense, or religious symbolism

Helping their parents prepare to host a church service, two boys place *Ausbund* hymnals on benches they have arranged in the second floor of their barn. *Credit: Burton Buller*

other than the plain clothing that all the worshippers are wearing. "Having churches in our homes helps mesh the sacred and secular," one minister has written. "The room where God was worshiped one day becomes our place of work the next day."[5]

Following the close of the worship service everyone stays for a simple noon meal provided by the family hosting church, and visiting continues through the afternoon. The lunch menu is dictated by local custom, which discourages any competitive impulse to outdo a previous host.

Church leaders are selected through a process that combines group choice and divine intervention. Since ministers and deacons serve for life, vacancies occur only when someone dies or becomes incapacitated, or when a church district grows large enough to divide into two districts and the new district needs its own clergy. All baptized members, men and women, are invited to nominate a man to fill a leadership vacancy. No one campaigns for the job. In fact, if a man were to say that he thought he would be a good preacher, that bit of boasting would almost surely disqualify him! Indeed, the major qualification for leadership in the Amish church is not speaking ability or administrative skill but leading by example and demonstrating a faithful Amish way of life.

Individuals who receive a certain number of nominations (the number varies from one community to another) then make up a cohort that the Amish call "the lot" because these men will draw lots to determine whom God is calling to fill the role. The tension in the room when the lots are drawn, in the presence of the gathered congregation, is palpable because everyone firmly believes that God is making the final selection. The one who is chosen cannot decline. He must submit to a new and heavy responsibility. He will receive no salary for his church work and will not attend seminary or receive any formal theological training apart from apprenticeship to more seasoned ministers in the church. Ministers, who preach and provide pastoral care in the congregation, and deacons, who collect and distribute alms and offering money to the elderly and to those with large medical bills, are all chosen in this way. Bishops, who bear overall responsibility for a church district and lead member meetings at which matters of church discipline are discussed, are also chosen by lot, but from the ranks of those already ordained ministers. Each church district typically has one bishop, two ministers, and one deacon.

The bishop plays a central role in the annual cycle of religious rituals. Twice each year, once in the spring and again in the autumn, the church district reaffirms fidelity to the Bible, renews its commitment to living within its Ordnung, and seeks to have any interpersonal disagreements resolved. In their sermons, the bishop and ministers stress the need for reconciliation within the church as a prerequisite for the church's observance of communion. In many other denominations, communion is a sign of an individual member's right relationship with God, but in Amish theology relationships with God and with one another are not easily separated. Only when each person believes he or she is at peace with everyone else, as well as with God, can communion move forward. The weeks preceding communion, then, are filled with visiting, confession, forgiving, and making amends. Participating in communion also signals one's submission to the dictates of the Ordnung.

Communion itself features a longer pattern of worship with sermons and other components that can stretch into the afternoon. Around 3:00 p.m., the time of day the Bible says Jesus died on the cross, the bishop breaks pieces of bread from a single loaf and distributes them to the members. He also passes a single cup of wine from which each member takes a sip. The bishop typically emphasizes that individual grains of wheat had to be ground into flour to make the communion bread and individual grapes crushed into wine, representing the submission and giving up of self-centeredness that is at the heart of Amish faith. The service ends with a ritual of foot washing, following the example of Jesus who washed his disciples' feet in the manner of a servant. As the congregation sings, members divide into pairs (men with men and women with women) and wash one another's feet in small tubs of water that the deacon has arranged.

Joining and Leaving

Although children brought up in Amish homes are nurtured in the Amish way and their parents hope and pray that they will profess faith and embrace the church, they are not members of the church until they ask to be baptized. At that point they become members, responsible to live faithfully by the Ordnung and to assist other members in practical and financial ways. The choice to join the church is a major decision and not one to be taken lightly. Since it is bound up with a clutch of other choices—whom to marry, where to make a home, and what kind of work one might pursue—the choice for baptism is often made in late adolescence or young adulthood. Those seeking baptism attend a series of catechism classes with the district ministers and are typically baptized in the spring, as part of a regular church service, indoors with water being poured over their heads. Although it is quite possible for someone who was raised in a very different context or religious tradition to join the Amish church, few people have done so.

The Amish view the vows of baptism, made on bended knee before God and to the church, to be the ultimate promise one can make and one with eternal consequences. Despite these stakes—and in part because of them—they also make provision for those who betray their promise and who, despite the best of intentions, at times forget, fall short, or wander from the Amish way. Confession and, if appropriate, restitution to injured parties, is the most common form of discipline and accountability. Confession might be made for sin named in the Bible, such as adultery or filing a lawsuit, or it might be made for expressing pride and self-centeredness through flouting of the Ordnung, such as purchasing some forbidden technology or going to a casino. Minor matters are confessed privately to the ministers, but more serious matters—determined by local custom—involve a public confession in church.

For individuals who refuse to confess, show no remorse, or who obviously wish to break with the church as evidenced by persistent nonattendance at worship or, for example, buying a car and moving out of state, the stakes are clear. Such individuals, after being repeatedly invited to repent and return, are excommunicated. Excommunication is never a surprise and it is quite rare because few people who might contemplate leaving the church ever join in the first place. But when excommunication occurs it is serious. In addition to being denied access to the rituals of the church, such as communion, the person is subject to shunning.

Because the Amish believe that church membership has practical, social implications, leaving the church also has social dimensions. Shunning is the ritualized recognition that a relationship has been broken and that things will not be the same unless the relationship is righted. Shunning does not mean that other Amish cannot have anything to do with the excommunicated person or cannot speak with him or her. It does mean that members will avoid the person in certain symbolic ways, such as not sharing a meal together and not entering into business contracts with them. Depending on the circumstances that surrounded an individual's exit and excommunication, family, friends, or the individual may feel deeply betrayed. In such situations, the practice of shunning may inadvertently become more exaggerated and bitter. In other situations, the person who has been excommunicated remains on good terms with other Amish people, but still observes the boundaries shunning has imposed in ways not unlike a couple in mainstream society whose divorce proceeding

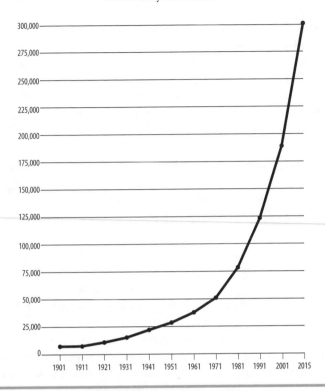

Fig. 4.2. Amish Population Growth in North America, 1901–2015 *Source: Raber's New American Almanac, 1930–2015; The Mennonite Year Book, 1905–1960; Amish historical documents.*

was amiable but who nevertheless adheres to the child custody rules set down by a judge.

It is always possible for those who are excommunicated and shunned to rejoin the Amish church. Such cases have occurred, even many years after the original falling out. But those cases are quite rare. Generally, by the time a person has been excommunicated, he or she has considered—often over the course of months if not years— the implications of the choice. Those who leave cite a variety of reasons. For those in middle age, the chief reason is often a desire to be part of a church with a different theological or spiritual emphasis— perhaps one with an evangelical or Pentecostal flavor. For younger people, the lure of forbidden technology or the pursuit of higher education is more often a factor, while in other cases young people who leave are seeking to distance themselves from a dysfunctional or abusive Amish home.

Either way, the number of people who are excommunicated and shunned (that is, who leave *after* having joined the church) is very small. More common is a young person raised in an Amish home who never requests baptism and gradually drifts away. Such individuals are often said to have left the Amish, but since they were never members of the church in the first place, they are not excommunicated or shunned and are free to visit and share meals with their Amish relatives. Such young people may join another denomination or none at all. Their parents are no doubt disappointed with their choice to forego Amish baptism, but shunning does not complicate the relationship in these cases.

The story of leaving the church is a dramatic one, often full of pain and pathos, and has been the subject of both thoughtful memoires and error-filled exposés. But the larger story is one of children joining their parents' church and remaining contented and productive members for their entire lives. Nationally 85 percent or more of those born to Amish parents join the church. Almost all of the remaining 10 to 15 percent had never joined in the first place, and only a thin slice had joined and was subsequently excommunicated.[6]

The retention rate of 85 percent surprises observers who assume that the Amish church would not prove attractive to children growing up with increasing awareness of the opportunities and possibilities available in the wider world. Amish parents profess less surprise, believing that the trade-off for loss of individual freedom is community, security, and purpose. Either way, the dynamics of that decision can be complicated, as chapter 5 explains.

CHAPTER FIVE

Rumspringa:
Amish Gone Wild?

"KATE'S LIKE A LOT OF AMERICAN TEENAGERS," RE-marked Pennsylvania journalist Gil Smart. "She likes country music. She lists her favorite TV shows as 'One Tree Hill' and 'Friday Night Lights.' And she's on Facebook, with more than 200 Facebook 'friends.'" What made Kate and her friends newsworthy was a piece of the story Smart had not expected to uncover: Kate was—at least judging by her dress—Amish. Unlike Kate, most of her Amish Facebook friends did not post pictures of themselves in Amish clothes. They appeared in backwards baseball caps and muscle shirts or with jewelry and makeup. They followed celebrities and commented on pop culture. And they sometimes posted selfies with friends at parties in which most people appeared inebriated.[1]

What is going on here? By 2011, when Smart came across Kate's profile, Facebook was ubiquitous and claimed half a billion members. But a connection to Amish youth surprised observers and reminded others of similarly jarring news stories in which Amish teens were shown to be doing things that diverged sharply from their parents' lifestyle. In 1998 when two Amish-reared young men in southeastern Pennsylvania were arrested with intent to distribute cocaine for the Pagans motorcycle gang the story had caused an international media sensation.

These sorts of revelations have made *Rumspringa*—the Pennsylvania Dutch word for "running around," which the Amish use to describe teen socializing—one of the most well-known, yet misunderstood, aspects of Amish life. Television reality shows, TV dramas such as *Judging Amy*, and a 2002 documentary called *The Devil's Playground* have all played up the Rumspringa theme, fueling both surprise and puzzlement. Although most of these media representations have been riddled with inaccuracies, America's confusion and fascination with Rumspringa are understandable. Why do straightlaced parents allow their children this sort of freedom? What does Rumspringa entail, and how does it not become a simple exit ramp out of Amish life?

Teens Gone Wild?

When Amish teens reach the age of sixteen or seventeen they enter a life stage known in Pennsylvania Dutch as Rumspringa, which stretches until baptism or marriage (depending on the particular Amish subgroup). Inaccurately labeled a "time out," Rumspringa has been depicted as a ritual in which Amish parents send their teens out into the world as a sort of testing to see how many will prove faithful and return. Nothing could be further from the truth. In no way do parents encourage their children to engage in deviant behavior, nor do they send them away. Rumspringa, as we'll see, is an adolescent rite of passage, and some parents take a more hands-off approach to parenting their teens than do others. But no Amish church or household urges their youth to sample the temptations of the world as a means of deciding whether they wish to join the Amish church.

Amish teens do not move to New York apartments or California beach houses, despite what the reality TV series *Amish in the City* contended. Rumspringa-age youth live at home with their parents and siblings. Their social life is more independent from the rest of their family. They spend weekend evenings with Amish peers of

The peer group is the focus of socializing during Rumspringa. These teens in Shipshewana, Indiana, spend a summer evening together in town rather than with their parents and younger siblings. *Credit: Don Burke*

their own age, known as *Die Youngie* (young folks), rather than with their parents' friends or their younger brothers and sisters.

Nor are Rumspringa-age youth breaking church rules or at risk of being shunned. Since they have not been baptized and are not members of the church, they cannot be excommunicated. They have not yet committed themselves to the Amish way as adults. Parents hope and pray that their children will make that choice. But until teens request baptism, they are not bound by the regulations of the church any more than their English neighbors are.

So what is Rumspringa? As a distinct phase in the Amish life cycle, Rumspringa is shaped by a mix of Amish social structure, theology, and tradition. The structure of Amish society includes two principal authorities: the family and the church. During the later teen years, Amish youth live betwixt and between these two authorities.

A young person begins to move out from under the authority of his or her parents (following old rural customs in which sixteen-year-olds begin to gain some degree of autonomy), but is not yet under the authority of the church (because he or she has not yet been baptized). These years are a liminal time in which teens have more independence than they have had as children and more freedom than they will have after, presumably, they join the church.

An Amish theology of adult baptism ties the hands, to some degree, of parents and ministers in controlling behavior in the late teen years. At the same time, long-standing rural traditions of youthful "running around" with one's peer group on weekend evenings lend weight to the idea that turning sixteen (or seventeen in more conservative affiliations) marks the beginning of a rite of passage toward adulthood.

Amish Adolescence

One feature of Amish adolescence that is sometimes lost in all the breathless descriptions of Rumspringa by outsiders is that Amish teens spend a great deal of time working and bear significant responsibilities for running family farms and businesses. Amish children end their formal schooling at age fourteen or fifteen and thereafter are engaged full time in farm, house, or shop work. State labor laws keep them from taking full-time employment beyond the family setting, but there is usually enough work at home to keep them busy or they might work for a relative on a part-time basis. In any case, Amish teens bear remarkable responsibilities that would be unusual for those their age in the English world. A fifteen-year-old girl may manage her mother's dry goods store several days a week, handling sales, managing inventory, and preparing wholesale orders. A sixteen-year-old boy, having learned hydraulics repair skills in his father's shop, may be given major off-site repair jobs and be expected to advise non-Amish clients on their equipment needs and upgrades. In this sense, Amish adolescents function, in many ways, with decidedly adult responsibilities.

At the same time, Amish youth are in the process of becoming their own person. That process, however, is colored by Amish culture. In Western societies imbued with the belief that individualism

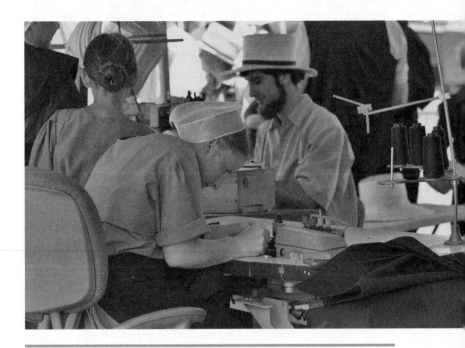

Amish adolescents are given adult work responsibilities. *Credit: Daniel Rodriguez*

is a virtue, many people assume that adolescents develop their identity as they become autonomous. Psychologist Richard Stevick argues that for the Amish, and other collectivist cultures, that connection is not so obvious. The values of Gelassenheit, cooperation, and obedience discourage autonomy, and Amish parents and teachers rarely if ever encourage independence. Having grown up with distinctive dress and horse-drawn transportation reinforcing one's identity on every childhood trip to town, identity and autonomy for Amish teens are actually in tension with one another.

A key question for Amish youth, then, is how they will understand their personal identity in the context of the group. For the vast majority, that question hinges on connecting with an Amish peer group apart from the extended family and finding a mate so as to establish one's own adult household within Amish society. Rumspringa provides a space to pursue these goals.

In popular media portrayals of Rumspringa, an emphasis is often placed on the question of whether a young person will join the church or leave the community for good. This sort of question may plague a few Amish teens, but for the vast majority, the decision to join the church is assumed. Outsiders like to ponder how *they* would respond to such a high-stakes choice, and have made this sort of existential struggle the central theme in novel plots and movie scripts featuring Amish characters. But for Amish teens, the focus is on developing a peer group and finding a marriage partner. "Running around" alludes to this element of peer socialization.

This does not mean that there is no anxiety wrapped up in Rumspringa years. For some teens, a fear of dying before they have joined the church—and the possibility that they might therefore end up in hell—is terrifying. For others, lack of information about the dangers of alcohol and drugs has deepened the consequences of experimentation with such substances.

Innocent Fun and Deviant Behavior

What the relative freedom of Rumspringa means varies greatly from one community to another, and even from one family or one individual to another. In some settlements and among some affiliations, youth activities are closely monitored by parents, while in other settings, teens are given freer range. Many teens spend these years doing very little that their parents or ministers would not approve. Others engage in deviant behavior—from an Amish perspective—such as going to the movies or wearing non-Amish clothing. Boys often take such deviance further than girls, and it is not uncommon, in many places, for a Rumspringa boy to obtain a driver's license and buy a car— usually from another Amish boy who is selling his car because he intends to join the church! A percentage of Amish youth spend these years in more reckless behaviors, such as underage drinking or sexual promiscuity. In no case do parents "send" or encourage their children into such activity.

One of the central features of Rumspringa, regardless of the nature of the activity one chooses, is finding a specific Youngie peer group, known as one's "crowd" or "buddy bunch." In small settlements, the community's entire age cohort may constitute this group. In large settlements, with a thousand or more Amish teens, different groups, each with its own nickname and reputation, form. A sixteen-year-old may join a group based on the recommendation of an older sibling or a school friend, or with an eye to the group's general reputation in the community. Some groups may be known for engaging in rowdy behavior while others are reputed to be quite tame.

Some socializing is done in single-sex crowds. Teen boys in some settlements participate in softball leagues, go fishing, or play ice hockey. A 2012 article in *Runner's World* described a group of twenty or so Amish young men in Lancaster, Pennsylvania, who—wearing top-of-the-line running shoes but also "black pants held up with suspenders and long-sleeve, button-down shirts"—regularly run half marathons, largely for the camaraderie.[2]

Most Rumspringa activity is mixed gender and can include birding, which is popular in the Midwest, and volleyball, which is popular everywhere. Some Amish refer to volleyball as their national pastime. Requiring little expensive equipment and open to people of varying skill levels, it can be played in pastures, lawns, and parks. Volleyball nets can be strung from designated poles, trees, and even parked buggies.

One youth activity with a long tradition and present in virtually every settlement is the Sunday night singing. In most places, youth gather on a Sunday evening at the home of the family that hosted church that morning. The evening begins with singing German hymns in the slow cadence used in morning worship. Soon the tempo increases, unison gives way to four-part harmony, and the songs switch to English, often gospel songs such as "Amazing Grace," "When the Roll Is Called up Yonder," or "Will the Circle Be Unbroken?" Snacks may be served at intervals and there can be social chatter between songs. Occasionally, to the chagrin of the evening's hosts, members of a rowdy Youngie group may appear to heckle or otherwise interrupt the hymn singing. The evening of singing culminates with conversations—some preplanned, some spontaneous, some awkward—in which young men ask to escort young women home. These sorts of contacts constitute a typical (though not universal) public indication of courtship.

Apart from a Saturday afternoon of volleyball or a Sunday evening of singing, some Amish crowds (especially in large settlements where even a small percentage of "wild" teens can translate into a

Volleyball is a popular social activity for Amish young people in many communities. *Credit: Daniel Rodriguez*

sizable number of people) plan raucous parties. They may hire a band, bring a dozen kegs of beer, and draw several hundred participants. Observers suggest that men outnumber women at such parties three to one. In a twist on typical Amish aversion to engaging law enforcement to settle disputes, some parents who learn of such parties and are fearful of the possibility they hold for heavy drinking or even drug use have been known to call the sheriff on their children. (The Amish are not, traditionally or on the whole, teetotalers, so drinking alcohol itself is often not seen as a problem so much as drunkenness.)

In the New Order affiliation, and among many others, especially in smaller settlements, the social life of the Youngie is quite restricted and closely monitored. Dating takes place only at home and in the presence of parents, and adult chaperones accompany larger youth groups to evening volleyball games.

The presence of Amish teens on Facebook, made possible in some large and relatively progressive settlements by the presence of smart phones which allow youth to log on to social media even though their homes do not have electricity or Internet service, suggests one difficulty parents face: most of them are largely unfamiliar with Facebook or with other social media and web-based technology. To be sure, social media has not penetrated every Amish settlement, nor is its presence universal in the places that it has. But the photos, language, and connections that some of the Youngie post on Facebook and Instagram are much more easily hidden from today's parents than is an alcohol-laced party in the woods. Such hoedowns, while clearly frowned upon, have been around for generations and elders have some idea of what they are dealing with. Not so with the new social media.

Some of the Youngie's postings would shock their elders. At the same time, since Amish kids on Facebook are generally only "friends" with other Amish youth, the Rumspringa foray into Facebook illustrates one of the critical yet often overlooked aspects of Rumspringa generally: activities during this phase of Amish life, even those that the Amish deem deviant, generally reinforce group identity. Although Rumspringa raises eyebrows among onlookers, and Amish parents of wayward youth may worry through sleepless weekend nights, the practice actually insulates Amish youth from the world. Even when Rumpsringa groups engage in deviant activities, they do so as sizable and identifiable groups of Amish youth, not as lone individuals swallowed up in an English crowd.

It's perhaps no surprise, then, that the vast majority of teens end their Rumspringa years in the same way they have seen so many older members of their peer group do so: requesting baptism, moving under the discipline of the church, and marrying.

Courtship and Marriage

The Amish have never had arranged marriages or any sort of parental matchmaking. Young people are free to identify mates within the Amish community, although both individuals must become members of the church to be married in the church. Baptism, then, can be a sign that one is getting serious about settling down. In some affiliations, including among the New Orders, dating is only allowed for those who have already joined the church—a practice that leaves dating teens subject to church rules rather than parental discretion.

Courtship practices are one area of Amish life where there is a great deal of variation from place to place, sometimes as a result of differing old customs and sometimes due to the way even common patterns have evolved along different lines over the years. Traditional customs, which continue to be presented in tourist venues operated by English entrepreneurs, involve couples keeping their relationships secret, even from their parents, until the prospective son-in-law approaches a girl's father with a marriage proposal. Such secrecy persists in a few places, but is no longer typical. Likewise, the practice of "bundling," whereby a couple spends a good portion of the night, fully clothed, in the young woman's bed, is also quite rare nowadays. Not surprisingly, this custom, which was practiced by New England Puritans and many other northern European immigrant groups, provoked a great deal of tongue wagging and more than a few sermons from Amish ministers through the years. The widely reported story that Amish parents paint fence gates blue to signal they have a marriageable daughter ready to begin dating has never been true. It is a pure myth, through and through.

In some communities it is common and expected for individuals to date several people during their Rumspringa years, some casually and others more seriously. In other settlements courting itself signals a serious relationship, and consent to date is all but tantamount to engagement. In some very conservative affiliations, much courting is done via letter writing, even if the two parties live quite close to one another.

Although keen observers of Amish society know that there are cases of physical abuse in Amish homes, they also note the near absence—compared with patterns in wider U.S. society—of physical aggression on the part of Amish young men toward their girlfriends. In more than a quarter century of work with Amish youth, one psychologist had never "heard of a single case of an Amish young man hitting or beating up his girlfriend," despite hearing from individuals who freely shared other painful experiences and sensitive information. Although he believes there must be some cases, he "is convinced that they occur far less frequently . . . than [among] mainstream American youth," and hypothesizes that the "teaching and example of Gelassenheit, coupled with minimal exposure to violent media" contribute to this positive pattern of behavior.[3]

There are various traditions surrounding marriage proposals. In some places, proposals are made through a "second"—often a good friend of the prospective groom. In other cases, the young man will ask the deacon of the church district in which the young woman lives to ask her and her parents. Once a couple agrees to marry, planning and preparation for hosting and feeding hundreds of wedding guests begin. In the Kalona, Iowa, settlement, and a few other places, the young man may take up residence in his future parents-in-law's home as the wedding approaches so as to lend a hand with the work involved in getting everything ready to host the big event.

The average age of marriage in Amish circles is 21 for women and 22 for men. And almost everyone marries: more than 90 percent of people over age thirty are wed (or have been widowed). Wedding details vary from one settlement to another, but they share a number of common attributes. The wedding ceremony does not highlight the creativity or originality of the couple. Instead it sets the husband and wife in the church-community context of which they will be a part, it reaffirms tradition by following prescribed elements and resisting innovation, and it highlights the role of the church in providing a kind of sacred canopy over all of Amish life. There are no photographs, gowns, or rings. The couple wears new clothes, but not different in color or style from what they would wear to church on Sunday. Typically there are four attendants (two men and two women) who are friends of the bride and groom and who constitute the wedding party.

In the Lancaster, Pennsylvania, settlement and communities stemming from it, weddings are most often held from late October to early December and again in March, while in some other places June is a common month. Weddings typically take place on a weekday and are held in the bride's home or the home of one of her relatives. Because the wedding hosts will use the church district's benches for seating guests, it is difficult to have a wedding on a Monday or Saturday, since that would involve hasty movement of benches between

A decorated *Eck*, or bridal corner, at a wedding reception in northern New York. The newly married couple sits here with their attendants for an afternoon of eating and visiting. *Credit: Karen M. Johnson-Weiner*

the homes hosting church and hosting the wedding. Midweek weddings make those logistics easier.

Weddings follow a format similar to that of a Sunday morning worship service, with prescribed hymns, prayers, and lengthy sermons. Sermons usually look at the joys and the pitfalls of family life as revealed in the stories of biblical families, such as Isaac and Rebecca. Almost always there is a retelling of the story of Tobit, a Hebrew book not included in English Protestant Bibles but usually included in German translations of Scripture. Tobit does right by marrying someone from his own people, a choice that affirms the Amish practice of endogamy, or marriage within the group. Although the Amish forbid the marriage of close relatives, and marriage partners are rarely from the same church district, finding an Amish mate—and usually one from the same affiliation—is expected.

At the end of the three-hour service, the bishop calls the bride and groom forward for the five-minute exchange of vows and declaration of marriage. The rest of the day is spent with a series of bountiful meals provided for the several hundred guests in attendance.

The newlyweds typically spend the day after the wedding helping to clean up from the big event—taking down benches, scrubbing floors, and the like. There are no elaborate honeymoon plans, though couples may take several weeks to several months visiting extended family before moving into their own place. As married members of the Amish community they have now established their own household and are expected to assume their responsibilities as adults. One of those responsibilities is to create a home for children and to raise them in the faith.

CHAPTER SIX

Family and Schooling

"WE HOLLER, WE SHIVER, WE JUMP, WE SCREAM, WE cheer, and we groan." Loren Beachy, a young man from the Amish settlement in Elkhart and LaGrange Counties, Indiana, was describing an evening playing Pictionary with family and friends. On this particular April evening Aunt Inez and her husband, Andrew, had invited nieces and nephews and those young folks' friends for supper. After dinner Inez asked the guests if they would sing, and they obliged with a number of English gospel songs. Although there had been joking and friendly banter all evening, when the group divided into three teams around the table to compete at drawing and guessing words such as *wag, tidal wave,* and *moccasin,* the laughter and teasing rose to a whole new level: "Calvin is our artist for *beg.* Simple word, right? But try drawing it so your partners can guess it in a minute flat!"

For Loren and the others, it was a memorable evening, but not an unusual one. Gathering for dinner, singing together, visiting, and playing indoor or outdoor games is standard Amish fare. Family groupings that span the generations are often central to such occasions, but the inclusion of neighbors and friends—especially if the get-together includes teens or young adults—is assumed. In this case, the Pictionary teams were gender segregated. That arrangement is not always the case, but on this evening Loren thought the friendly gender rivalry generated much of the energetic laughter as the women were "breathing down our necks" and the teams swapped the lead as they moved around the board.[1]

In addition to kinship and neighborhood, there was yet another connection that linked this group. A number of the young adults were teachers in Amish schools. They had attended teacher meetings together, exchanged lesson plans, and shared schoolroom joys and frustrations. On this evening, church, family, school, and community overlapped, as they do so often in the high context culture of Amish life. These institutions reinforce one another and work together to pass on the faith to the next generation, and family and school play the most prominent roles in this regard.

Amish at Home

The home is a key space in Amish society. It is not only a center of family life, but also—as we've seen—the location of church services and weddings. Funerals also take place in the home of the deceased. For members of more traditional affiliations, such as the Swartzentruber Amish or Andy Weaver Amish, a great deal of canning and food preservation takes place with the aim of making the home as self-sufficient as possible. For those in relatively more progressive affiliations, where store-bought staples are common, the home is still at the center of production for households that are farming or operating a family business. Amish parents laugh at the overly idyllic image, served up by tourist brochures, of Amish homes as quiet, serene places—"With six children ten and under!" one mother remarked. But there is a sense in which Amish homes, due to their rural settings and their more limited technology, are free of what is, in other settings, assumed to be normal background noise.

Furniture is generally spartan by the standards of mainstream America, although some households in larger and more liberal

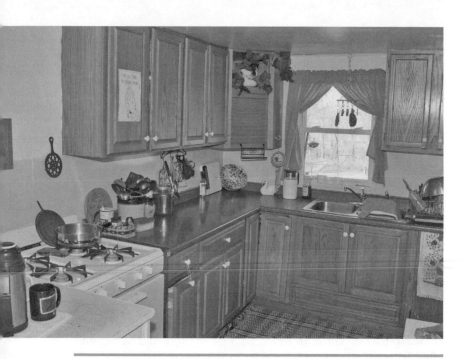

A kitchen in a moderately progressive Amish community features attractive cabinetry and gas-powered appliances. Kitchens in more conservative affiliations have wood stoves, iceboxes, and no indoor plumbing. *Credit: Don Burke*

settlements have comfortable recliners, beautiful kitchen cabinetry, and lovely grandfather clocks. But even here there is no wall-to-wall carpeting. More conservative households simply have rough wood or linoleum flooring throughout, while those at the other end of the spectrum may have more expensive hardwood flooring and area rugs of various kinds. In line with the values of humility, there is no portrait photography on display. Most Amish families do not have family photos, while those from more progressive affiliations might have photos—even albums, in some cases—but do not display them.

The language of the home is a German dialect commonly known as "Pennsylvania Dutch," or *Pennsilfaanisch Deitsch*. The dialect is not confined to Pennsylvania, and Amish people across the country speak Pennsylvania Dutch, although there is some variation in vocabulary and pronunciation from region to region. Unless an outsider is present, conversation is virtually always carried out in Pennsylvania

Dutch. Amish people read and write in English, so letters or notes left on a kitchen table are in English even as the verbal conversation throughout the day is in the dialect. In that sense, the Amish home is bilingual: German dialect for spoken communication and English for written. In addition, a select number of religious texts—Martin Luther's translation of the Bible, the *Ausbund* hymnal, a prayer book—are read in standard High German, but almost no one speaks High German conversationally.[2]

Growing Up Amish

Amish communities are full of children. Married women on average have about seven children, which means that the typical Amish person has six siblings, twenty-four aunts and uncles, and eighty-four first cousins. The Amish view infants as innocent and vulnerable, and delight in and even dote on babies. At the same time, parents believe that one of their primary tasks is to instill a sense of discipline in their children. Young children are given responsibility for chores around home and taught to obey both mother and father. Although gender roles are clear to children, chores are not rigidly defined by sex. Boys may be asked to help take care of the baby and girls might be enlisted in the barn, for example. Chores change with the seasons and also vary from one affiliation to another. For example, during the winter, Swartzentruber Amish need to cut and store ice in straw-insulated ice houses for use in the summer. (Most other Amish have natural gas–powered refrigerators.) Amish children grow up around animals, and caring for pets is a responsibility that usually begins at a young age. Even families that do not live on a farm have a driving horse, which older children help feed and water.

When children begin first grade they enter a new stage in life. School-age boys and girls are called "scholars." There is no gender segregation in Amish schools or school curricula, and boys and girls often share in the same games and activities at recess. After completing eighth grade, teens work at home and begin to take on more distinct gender roles that point to adulthood. A boy may begin working full time in a woodworking shop or apprenticing as a welder, while his sister may spend much of her day canning food, sewing, or working in an aunt's quilt shop. Typically, until Amish youth are twenty-one they turn over their wages to their parents—who, in turn, provide for their needs and promise to give them financial help of various sorts when they marry and start a household of their own.

Gender Dynamics

Amish families are patriarchal in the sense that the Amish believe that the Bible teaches that the man is the head of the home and bears final responsibility for making major decisions that affect the household. In public settings, on a shopping trip to town, for example, this sense of patriarchal propriety might be expressed by a husband speaking for the family or doing most of the talking. At home, however, or with close friends, husbands and wives both speak freely and joke or banter, and although many household jobs are identified with one gender or another, most tasks are, at some point, undertaken jointly or by the other spouse if time and need demand. Some scholars have described such systems as "soft patriarchy," a set of gender norms that relaxes and flexes depending on the situation.

Amish publications often use the language of "marriage partners" to describe their ideal of complementary marriage. Women's work is valued as a contribution to a stable and thriving home. Married women with young children almost never accept employment away from home, but some women begin small retail stores or other small businesses from their homes. These firms typically grow out of the traditional women's realm of work—selling food, fabric, crafts, or greenhouse plants—but the sophistication of the businesses, and the fact that some of them end up employing their husbands, point to the economic and entrepreneurial room to maneuver that Amish women have. Lawyers and accountants who work with Amish clients report that it is uncommon for an Amish man to make major decisions about a farm or a family business without the close consultation of his wife.

The changing world of Amish work, which we explore in the next chapter, has unsettled family life in some ways. When most households were farming, patterns of intergenerational and men's and women's work were more fluid, running together depending on

Men and women work together preparing soft pretzels and other food for a benefit auction. Gender roles are traditional yet flexible depending upon the particular needs of a situation. *Credit: Daniel Rodriguez*

the season or the weather. As more men have taken jobs off the farm, family life runs the risk of becoming divided. Home alone with young children, wives of day-laboring men have found themselves inhabiting a narrowing domestic sphere, while their husbands may share fewer household chores and be less involved with child-rearing than before.

Outsiders with close contacts in the Amish world attest to vast numbers of happy marriages but know that difficult and dysfunctional relationships also exist. Church leaders are not oblivious to these situations, but the response of the church is shaped by competing cultural values. The Amish consider all violence and abuse to be sin, but they are also predisposed to encourage submission and patience. Bishops and ministers in some communities have launched homespun marriage seminars, sometimes under the rubric of "Family Helpers," in which they seek to smooth patriarchy's sharp edges, while upholding traditional understandings of the home. A question posed at such a gathering in Ohio in 2007 suggests the pain one woman felt. "I am very discouraged," the anonymous writer began. "When we go away, like to church, instead of helping with the little ones, my husband will scold me for not being ready. Often times by the time I get in the buggy I'd rather cry than go anywhere." The bishop's public answer, in turn, illustrates his effort to invoke the values of Gelassenheit and apply them to the husband, chiding him for thinking only of himself and putting his desires ahead of his family's needs: "The husband you describe here is not giving himself for you as Christ gave himself for the church. Your husband might be doing what he saw his father do unaware of how much this hurts you. He is thinking of himself more than he is thinking of you and he is not being a Godly leader. . . . The husband needs to help with the children and a Godly husband will."[3]

The Amish church forbids divorce, and a spouse who files for divorce, for any reason, risks excommunication. In cases of spousal abuse, ministers might suggest separation, but they may be slower to offer such counsel than would advisers in mainstream society. If husband or wife leaves the church and the other spouse does not, the person remaining Amish is expected not to remarry, holding open the possibility that the errant party could repent and return. If an Amish person is widowed, he or she will typically remarry quickly, especially if there are young children in the home. Across the board Amish people believe that children are best reared in a home with two parents.

Not all Amish fit easily into the standard Amish family structure. Those who never elect baptism and leave the faith are disproportionately men, which means that single women comprise a small but noticeable segment of many communities. Some single women embrace their status. They might develop businesses or travel with a degree of freedom that would be unlikely for a married woman, or form especially close relationships with their nieces and nephews. For others, singleness is marginalizing. They may feel obligated to devote themselves to caring for aging parents. Such care is valued and honored in Amish society, but it can also be a lonely place in a community that assumes marriage and children.

At the End of Life

It is rare for an elderly Amish person to be placed in a nursing home. Only if ongoing medical care is unusually technical will a person move into a professional care setting. Most often, members of the older generation move into a *Dawdyhaus* (grandfather's house) next to their children and grandchildren. They continue to be part of a multi-generational household, do odd jobs around the farm or family business, and perhaps assist with child care.

When death occurs, the wider community moves into action, taking over family chores, digging the grave, and attending to other details to allow the immediate family time and space to grieve. Licensed funeral directors play a small role, completing death certificates and performing basic embalming but not applying cosmetic enhancements or selling expensive caskets. Bodies are quickly returned to the deceased's home where family members of the same sex dress the body and place it in a simple coffin, made by an Amish carpenter. In the three days preceding the funeral, hundreds of people may come to view the body and extend sympathy to family members.

Church members bring benches to the home of the deceased and arrange them for the funeral service, which may draw three to six hundred people. Sometimes two or three services are conducted simultaneously in neighboring homes if there are more mourners than can crowd into one house. Funeral services do not focus on eulogizing the dead, but on expressing gratitude to God for life and recognizing that everyone's time on earth will, at some point, come to an end. "Mom used to say funerals are not just to bury the dead, but to remind us we must all face death," one middle-aged man remembered his mother telling him as a child.[4]

Following the service, the family proceeds to an Amish cemetery for the burial where the values of humility and equality are symbolized by the headstones. Regardless of one's status, age, or gender, they are all the same small size and engraved only with the individual's name, age, and birth and death dates. For months thereafter, a widow or widower can expect visitors every Sunday afternoon and evening, sharing memories and words of encouragement.

Small headstones with simple inscriptions express values of Gelassenheit even in death. *Credit: Don Burke*

Commitment to the aged is the corollary of Amish concern for maintaining spiritual fidelity with the past. "Perhaps one of the greatest spiritual teachings" he received from his parents and grandparents, reflected one Pennsylvania farmer in 2009, was how those generations "cared for their elderly parents." His grandparents had "provided living quarters for both [great-grandmothers] in their house and faithfully cared for them till they died . . . age 93 and 102." And then "we saw Dad's care for [our] grandparents" as they "cleaned grandparents' houses twice a year, cared for their gardens, did some of their sewing, got the estates ready for auction, repaired their broken furniture, and whatever, and read the Bible to them on Sundays."[5] These activities were critical pieces of the writer's spiritual formation, formation that was centered in the everyday activities of the home. Indeed, the routines and rituals of the home are critically important resources for bringing up children in the Amish way. In recent decades, parents have also had Amish schools to aid them in their efforts.

Who Shall Educate Our Children?

Until the mid-twentieth century virtually all Amish children attended public schools with non-Amish peers, under the instruction of non-Amish teachers. By the beginning of the twenty-first century, however, only a small portion of Amish children were enrolled in public schools (and these were clustered in a handful of settlements). The rise of Amish schools has been one of the most significant developments in the group's history.

Disaffection with public schools stemmed from three factors, all of which took on new significance as the 1900s wore on. First was the consolidation of rural one-room schools into larger and often town-based facilities. Amish parents preferred small-scale schools, within walking distance, that employed teachers who lived in the local community and knew the parents. Consolidated schools undercut these arrangements. Second, curricula were changing with the addition of science, health, and civics classes that sometimes included—or at least offered the opportunity to include—teaching of evolution, sex education, and patriotism, all of which met with Amish disapproval. Finally, state attendance laws began to override the informal patterns whereby farm kids, and especially boys, could end their schooling with eighth grade and continue their practical education through work experience at home through apprenticeship. As these developments accelerated, an Amish minister asked, "How can we parents expect our children to grow up untainted by the world if we voluntarily send them into a worldly environment, where they associate with worldly companions, and are taught by men and women not of our faith six hours a day, five days a week, for the greater part of the year?"[6]

Between the mid-1930s and the mid-1960s school authorities and Amish parents skirmished over schooling. Outcomes varied depending on the state or the degree to which either or both sides were willing to negotiate. In some places, fathers paid hefty fines and even sat in jail rather than send their children to high school. In other places, Amish parents bought abandoned one-room public schools and reopened them as private Amish schools. Sometimes public education officials approved these Amish schools and in other cases they moved to shut them down. Several conflicts ended up in court, notably one brought by officials in Green County, Wisconsin, that went all the way to the U.S. Supreme Court. In 1972 the high court ruled unanimously in *Wisconsin v. Yoder* that states must allow Amish children to end their formal education with eighth grade. Thereafter, most of the remaining conflicts were quickly resolved.

In the years that followed, the number of Amish schools shot up dramatically and an ever-increasing percentage of Amish children were enrolled in them. Today there are more than two thousand Amish schools enrolling students in grades one to eight. A handful of students (depending on the settlement) may complete a General Educational Development (G.E.D.) program after finishing eighth grade.

Most Amish schools are one- or two-room buildings with multiple grades in a single room. Older students are expected to help younger scholars and model good behavior. Since teaching happens in a common classroom, pupils in the lower grades absorb some of the lessons being taught to the older students across the room, which quietly prepares these youngsters for the future. Meanwhile, lessons directed to younger students review and reinforce learning for those in the upper grades who overhear the teacher's work with those in the lower grades.

The vast majority of Amish teachers are young Amish women who are themselves graduates of an eighth grade Amish school. Younger teachers learn from more experienced ones, and many attend regularly scheduled Amish teacher training workshops. Although Amish schools are a relatively new phenomenon, they have quickly become a unifying force and an Amish identity marker. Statewide gatherings of Amish school teachers and the writing of Amish school curricula, for example, have brought Amish people from various settlements and affiliations together in ways they had not connected before. Amish generally discourage homeschooling and in some settlements expressly forbid it. Homeschooling strikes Amish parents as an expression of go-it-alone independence, in contrast to their values of cooperation and fitting in with the larger group. Said one leader, "Children need the companionship of neighbors and

Teachers work with students across grade levels in a one-room Amish school.
Credit: Dottie Kauffmann/Mennonite Historical Library

friends to help develop" so they will "know how to get along with each other in later life."[7]

Purposeful Schooling

"We're not opposed to education," a Pennsylvania Amish school advocate asserted. "We're just against education higher than our heads. I mean education that we don't need."[8] Indeed, Amish parents insist on sending their children to school—absentee rates are low— but they believe that education always has a purpose and in their case, that purpose is to train children to be productive members of Amish society. The curriculum focuses on reading, writing, and mathematics. Some schools use older, discarded public school math and reading texts, but many more use one of several Amish-authored textbook series, such as the Pathway Readers or Study Time Mathematics.

Although Pennsylvania Dutch is children's first language, Amish schools are conducted in English because the Amish believe that

Baseball is a common recess game, played by boys and girls alike, at many Amish schools. *Credit: Don Burke*

being functionally bilingual is necessary for getting along in U.S. society. Amish students still practice penmanship and focus on English grammar to a degree that is uncommon in today's mainstream public and private schools. Many Amish schools also include some instruction for upper-grade students in reading High German, with a focus on the vocabulary and grammar specific to Luther's German translation of the Bible and other religious texts.

Religion as such is not a subject in Amish schools. There may be a short Bible reading and prayer at the beginning of the day and the class may sing several hymns. But formal instruction in Bible or doctrine is the purview of the church and the responsibility of parents, not young female school teachers. Nevertheless, Amish faith and values permeate the curriculum, from occasional church history stories included in the Pathway Readers to the way the school is organized and functions. For example, competition among children is not stressed; most activities are cooperative. Rather than charting and comparing how quickly individual students learn multiplication facts, for example, the emphasis is on an entire grade learning their math facts and on advanced students helping slower ones. Timed tests are quite rare, and students are told to take the time they need to do their best work rather than hurry. On the playground, teachers may intentionally mix teams each day to discourage ongoing competitive rivalry on the ball diamond or volleyball court.

Amish schools also reflect the range of Amish subgroups. Very conservative Swartzentruber communities, for example, focus on rudimentary learning and include more rote memorization than is common in other Amish schools. Amish schools from relatively more liberal communities favor more interactive pedagogies, often have colorful bulletin boards adorning the walls, and may put on short programs for parents and grandparents at Christmas and at the end of the school year during which students sing and recite poetry. These more progressive schools sometimes administer nationally standardized tests, and the results reveal proficiency in reading, writing, and math.[9] Indeed, measured in terms of occupational outcomes, Amish schooling seems quite adequate. Today graduates of eight-grade Amish schools operate thousands of thriving, profitable businesses across North America, as we'll see in the next chapter.

In the end, parents at all types of Amish schools judge their schools successful if they prepare hardworking youth with strong, practical skills. Amish education does not place youth on a track to become a lawyer or a concert pianist or a chemical engineer. From the perspective of modernity, those kinds of limits seem painfully parochial. From the Amish perspective, schools are doing what they should be doing when they work in harmony with family and church to cultivate disciplined, thoughtful, cooperative young people who will possess the inclination and the capacity to contribute to their community.

CHAPTER SEVEN

Work and Technology

UNDER BRIGHT SKIES AND WARM JULY SUN, THE twentieth annual Horse Progress Days opened in Arcola, Illinois, in 2013. The family of Vernon and Lizzie Ann Yoder hosted the event, which drew nearly 20,000 people—almost all of them Amish—to their 120-acre farm. The gathering, which rotates from one community to another, highlights new technology adapted for animal-powered equipment as well as "the latest equipment innovations" to show that horse farming "is possible, practical, and profitable."[1]

Each year Horse Progress Days features innovative products and at the 2013 event there was considerable buzz around a new technology known as ground-driven power-take-off. The technology uses the basic movement of horses and the wheeled cart they pull to generate enough revolutions per minute (RPM) to power hay mowers, hay balers, manure spreaders, and other farm equipment originally designed for use with power-take-off from a tractor motor. In short, the ground-driven variety allows farmers to operate fairly advanced equipment with no gasoline or diesel engine, not even a battery.

Planners recognized the irony of linking the term "progress" with an event that seems the epitome of old fashioned. "Agri-business people have made the word 'innovation' into something that is mainly used to market the latest and the greatest," one Ohio Amish man conceded. But "the word is also appropriately used to describe the [new] farming equipment the shop lads have come up with." In the case of the ground-driven power-take-off, the "shop lads" were I & J Manufacturing and White Horse Machine, both of Pennsylvania, and Wildcat Ridge Gears in Kentucky. These three firms are among several thousand Amish-run small businesses that have sprung up across the country in the past quarter century. In fact, if there is irony at Horse Progress Days, it is that the success of animal power farming has been spurred on by the entrepreneurial spirit of Amish who have moved *off* the farm and exchanged their plows for weekly paychecks as business people and day laborers.

Amish farming is far from dead. But agriculture has changed, and in most Amish settlements sizable majorities of families no longer till the soil—a change that has significant ramifications for Amish society. For those who continue to farm creatively, as well as for those who have moved into the world of shop work, technology looms large in shaping the contemporary definition of what it means to be Amish. The Amish have never rejected technology, but they use it on their own terms, terms that shape their lives and work in ways that reinforce their distinctive identity and separation from the world.

Down on the Farm

Until the later 1900s almost all Amish households worked the land. Farming was an esteemed way of life, according to one writer, because it put one in tune with "the natural order of daylight and dark, sunshine and rain, the swing of the seasons, and the blessings with which God has ordered our world." Compare this, he continued, "with the largely artificial environment of urban centers where night is well-lit, rain is the way to ruin a day, and food and fiber originate at the local store."[2]

Demonstrating an innovative two-way plow, manufactured by White Horse Machine Company, at the 2014 gathering of Horse Progress Days, Mount Hope, Ohio. *Credit: Douglas Scheetz*

In the mid-twentieth century Amish farms were typically small, diversified, and relied on family labor. Several cows, pigs, and chickens might complement forty to fifty acres of hay, corn, and wheat, along with a cash crop such as tobacco (in Lancaster, Pennsylvania) or peppermint (around Nappanee, Indiana). As mechanized tractor farming swept the countryside in the years after World War II, almost all Amish communities resisted. A handful of places—Kalona, Iowa; Haven, Kansas; Chouteau, Oklahoma; and a few others—adopted tractors, but the vast majority of Amish continued to till the soil with horses. (Those buying tractors, however, continued to use horse-and-buggy transportation on the road.)

Given the fact that farming functioned as an ideal occupation, Ordnung governing farm technology was especially slow to change. Tampering with tradition threatened to destroy the value that Amish people ascribed to farming in the first place. Yet as the years wore on, the realities of farming on a small scale proved more and more difficult economically and threatened to throw families off the land they loved. For example, as state health boards moved to require that milk be cooled in refrigerated bulk tanks, Amish dairymen faced a dilemma. In some places, such as Lancaster, Pennsylvania, they agreed to install tanks and refrigeration units powered by small diesel engines (rather than by public utility electricity). Among more conservative Amish affiliations, choices ran in different directions. They opted to retain milking by hand and cooling their milk by submerging their old-fashioned milk cans in cold water. But such choices meant that their milk could only be sold as Grade B for use in making cheese, which meant a lower price than that commanded by Grade A milk for drinking.

By the 1970s and 1980s the realities of the agriculture economy were putting a squeeze on small farmers. The Amish population was growing rapidly, while rising land prices, veterinary bills, and equipment, seed, and fertilizer costs were forcing young people to reconsider whether farming would be in their future. During these decades, in almost all Amish settlements, the number and percentage of households that moved into nonfarm jobs shot upward. Only about a third of families in Michigan, for example, were still farming in the early 2000s, about a quarter in western Pennsylvania's Lawrence County, and less than 20 percent in Holmes County, Ohio.

For the minority of Amish who remained on the land, the 1990s and early 2000s actually witnessed something of an agricultural renaissance. New technology, like that featured at Horse Progress Days, reduced costs and kept small-scale farming viable. In 2007 a detailed study in Geauga County, Ohio, that looked at horse and human labor required to farm found that on a per acre basis the financial return was considerably higher on Amish farms. Amish farms are much smaller, so the overall income was less than on a sprawling agribusiness spread. But with family labor and lower overhead costs in the Amish mix, farming with horses can be profitable.[3]

At the same time, a growing number of families have moved away from dairy and grain farming and into raising produce. Capitalizing on household labor and using wholesale produce auctions to get their products in the hands of restaurants and upscale grocery stores, a new generation of Amish farmers are able to support themselves growing tomatoes, peppers, broccoli, melons, and herbs. Other new agriculture initiatives include commercial fish farming, dairy goat herds, and the establishment of greenhouses offering retail and wholesale bedding plants and flowers.

Although many observers assume that Amish farms have always been all-organic producers, in fact during the course of the twentieth century most had begun using chemical herbicides and pesticides, to some degree, and adopted hybrid seeds and chemical fertilizers in addition to animal manure. The emergence of intensive produce farming, however, kick-started an Amish conversation about organic production—in some cases because non-Amish customers requested it, but also because "it was the right thing to do because it fit our beliefs," in the words of one Indiana farmer.[4] In 2003 a group of Amish produce farmers in Holmes County, Ohio, launched Green Field Farms as an organic marketing cooperative distributing vegetables, milk, and eggs. Today, more Amish farmers have gone organic than at any time in the recent past, but these producers still represent a minority of all Amish farms.

The Rise of Off-Farm Jobs

Amish agriculture is alive and well, but it represents a much smaller slice of the Amish occupational pie than it did in the 1950s. The shift away from farming has been the most significant change in Amish life since the group's arrival in North America, although the implications of that shift vary depending upon the type of work that has replaced plowing the fields. Work in factories, in construction trades, and in home-based manufacturing or retail shops have come to define the way most Amish people spend their work days.[5]

Nationally, employment in factories is the least common alternative to farming, but in some large settlements it is the norm. In northern Indiana's Elkhart-LaGrange and Nappanee settlements and in Geauga County, Ohio, jobs in industry have long been central to the Amish economy. In northern Indiana, more than half of working-age men punch a time clock, laboring in non-Amish-owned factories that build large recreational vehicles (RVs) and pop-up campers, which the Amish themselves would never purchase. In other settlements, Amish factory workers mass produce kitchen

An Amish worker attaches siding to a recreational vehicle in a factory in Elkhart County, Indiana. Half of working-age Amish men in north central Indiana are employed in non-Amish industry. *Credit: iStock/Scott Olson*

cabinets and garage doors, or labor on assembly lines with hot-rubber-extruding processes.

Industry may seem alien to Amish tradition, but it has come to fit some communities because it pays well, does not require high school credentials, and all the advanced equipment is owned by out-siders and is confined to the factory floor. An employee who drives a forklift or uses an inventory app on the company's iPad cannot use these items at home since they remain at the plant when the shift ends. Of course, such employment does introduce seeds of social change. Factory work is limited to forty hours a week and often includes paid vacation, thus giving employees much more leisure time than a farmer can ever enjoy. Moreover, most industry employs only men, meaning that work for them is separated from home and from intergenerational interaction. Finally, because such work does not require any investment on the part of the workers other than a lunch box, industry jobs pump disposable income into Amish communities that encourages consumer spending and perks like eating in restaurants that are not possible for farm families who need to reinvest profits back into the land.

Work in construction—carpentry, roofing, masonry, and more specialized trades—is a second area of external employment. Unlike factory work, it carries a legitimacy linked to tradition. Farmers in earlier generations often spent winter months operating sawmills or building furniture, and the skills associated with old-fashioned barn raisings (in which a group of builders erected a barn in a day) point to long-standing connections between Amish culture and construction. Yet today's world of custom building takes Amish labor in some very new directions. Like factory work, it is a male-dominated sector and Amish contractors and their employees spend very long days away from home—sometimes spending the night in distant motels when the job site is far from their community. Transportation to and from the construction area almost always requires a permanent relationship with one or more drivers who own or lease trucks and provide daily transport to urban and suburban worksites. Contractors were also among the first Amish to begin using cell phones to communicate with suppliers and subcontractors, and many have upgraded to smart phones. Church leaders wanted cell phones to remain turned off and in the truck after work hours, but contractors admit that doesn't always happen.

A World of Small Shops

By far the most common alternative to farming has been the creation of small shops. Since the mid-1970s a quiet industrial revolution has reshaped Amish society with as many as twelve thousand Amish-owned firms sprouting in settlements all across North America. Many are cottage industries that employ only a single family, while others are growth-oriented small businesses that employ five to thirty other people and have wider product lines and larger sales volumes. Amish businesses make, repair, and retail all sorts of things. There are furniture shops, leather works, welding shops, bicycle repair shops, small groceries, dry goods stores, auctioneers, butchers, and bookkeepers. Some focus on the Amish market, making carriages or

Signs for Amish enterprises near Salem, Arkansas, indicate no sales on Sundays, publicly acknowledging the moral boundaries of Amish business. *Credit: Don Burke*

felt hats, for example, while others cater to a non-Amish clientele, such as a quilt shop that draws on the tourist trade. A great many businesses span Amish and non-Amish markets.

Entrepreneurship is rooted in the cultural soil of Amish society, drawing on skills honed through years of self-employed and resourceful farming. Owners laud shops as the next best thing to farm life: these businesses often draw on the labor of the entire family, including children and grandparents, and because they are home based, such firms do not separate husbands from the rest of the household. In addition, Amish shops are under the control of the family, who can set the terms and conditions of work. Signs proclaiming "No Sunday sales" are ubiquitous and help stake out the religious boundaries of work. Production schedules can also flex to allow for time off to attend midweek weddings or to accommodate special days in their traditional religious calendar, such as Ascension Day (forty days after Easter) or Pentecost Monday. Such flexibility also allows them to work right through civic holidays, such as Memorial Day or Labor Day, that do not mean much to them.

Yet small business ownership brings its own set of challenges and changes. Families appreciate the fact that work is home based, but that characteristic means that negotiating technological change and navigating commercial demands also take place in the home itself. English-speaking customers, delivery drivers, and wholesalers engage children and adults on a regular basis. The pressures of production encourage the adoption of new technologies, not on a distant job site or factory floor but around hearth and home. The adage "the customer is always right" may reshape priorities and practices in subtle ways. Not least, many home-based businesses are financial successes, netting millions of dollars a year and presenting Amish families with the problem of wealth. Church Ordnung puts the brakes on conspicuous consumption—buggies are all roughly the same sort, for example, and jewelry is forbidden—but entrepreneurs' hunting cabins or winter apartments in Sarasota, Florida, offer retreats for the well heeled that set them apart.

Amish businesses succeed, in part, because of the cultural capital entrepreneurs bring to the workplace. Low overhead costs and family labor enhance the bottom line, as does the church's commitment to mutual aid. Health and liability insurance is provided by the church, releasing businesses from the inflated premiums charged by for-profit insurers. Amish employers and their Amish employees are exempt from Social Security and Medicare taxes (and, in some states, from workers' compensation).

Shops are also handicapped in some ways. For instance, they will almost never sue for damages, even when they have been shamelessly scammed, because of the church's insistence on defenselessness. As well, the church's general resistance to conspicuous size and scale means that larger businesses may have to strategically downsize if their growth offends people in the church. Although there is no formal protocol for such downsizing, Amish firms are sometimes scaled down or sold to non-Amish parties for reasons that make little sense from a business standpoint, but demonstrate the founder's submission to Amish values. Education and technology limits also bridle some firms. In most Amish groups, direct use of the Internet for advertising or merchandizing is not possible, and within a shop itself, the inability to tap public utility electricity indirectly caps growth.

At the same time, these sorts of technological limitations become, in their own way, an asset, helping to create a distinct Amish "brand." Low-tech production helps develop an Amish product mystique. The sense of value and distinctiveness that accompanies the Amish label is closely tied to the fact that the Amish have chosen to engage technology in highly distinctive ways.

Amish Tech

Popular images of the Amish paint them as Luddites or techno-phobes who shun any labor-saving device or advanced technology. Such an image is grounded in the fact that Amish people do often make strikingly different choices than do other Americans when it comes to technology. The Amish do not assume that faster is neces-sarily better, nor do they automatically equate the adjectives *new* and *improved*. They view all of life as falling under the sacred canopy of church Ordnung, and they assume that the faithful church will be, in many ways, distinguishable from "the world." These principles do not mean that the Amish employ a thoughtless reaction against innovation. Rather, they evaluate new technologies with an eye to how they will change their community or destabilize tradition, whereas most other Americans size up technology simply from the standpoint of efficiency and cost and assume that faster speeds and more options are always a good thing.

In fact, there are few pieces of technology that the Amish consider categorically out of bounds. Instead, they regard most technology as morally neutral and focus on how it might be used. A dishwasher, for example, is not "evil." But Amish families reject dishwashers because they eliminate household chores that parents believe are helpful exer-cises in training responsible, diligent children. In the same way, pub-lic utility electricity is problematic not because electricity in itself is wrong, but because wiring one's home with multiple outlets in every room announces that the home owner is ready and waiting—even eager—to plug in any new device on the market. It suggests that the decision to embrace whatever comes along is a foregone conclusion. Instead, as a consumer *community* the Amish believe that moral

This Amish woodworking shop uses equipment powered with hydraulic (oil) and pneumatic (air) pressure. *Credit: Daniel Rodriguez*

discernment must come first and that power arrangements—batteries for clocks, naphtha gas for lamps, propane for refrigerators, and so on—can follow later for those things deemed worthwhile.

A similar focus on the impact of technology rather than technology *per se* animates the common Amish distinction between use and ownership. From the Amish perspective, one of the common threats posed by technology is its ability to make individuals self-reliant and independent, thereby mocking the spirit of humility and making community optional. When a member rents something she or he might not be allowed to own, they give up a measure of control. A shop owner might lease a building with electric lights from a non-Amish property owner but not install such lighting in her own home, or a man might use a riding lawnmower as a groundskeeper for a non-Amish business but not buy and use such a mower himself. This distinction between use and ownership is, in many cases, vital to the dynamic nature of Amish entrepreneurship. But it also illustrates the deep assumptions the community holds about the perils of technology.

Given these deep assumptions, Amish approaches to technology span a gamut from rejection through adaptation to simple acceptance. A few entertainment technologies are banned outright, such as television. Meanwhile, a good number of basic household appliances and shop tools have been adopted and then adapted to operate without electricity. Households might use a diesel or solar powered air pump to raise water from a well or to run a sewing machine. Shop owners operate a host of manufacturing equipment, such as lathes and belt sanders, with hydraulic power. Batteries connected to alternating current inverters can power cash registers or photocopiers. Different affiliations draw the line at different places, with more conservative groups rejecting more and adapting less than progressive affiliations are inclined to do.

In more progressive settlements, the use of computers for managing company bookwork or running computer-aided design (C.A.D.) programs has been the focus of recent debate and discussion. While some firms have outsourced their computer work to an English associate, more common has been the adoption of computers that have a DSL line for email but no Internet, audio, or video capability. At least one Amish-owned business actually builds such machines for other Amish firms, who run them with batteries charged via solar or diesel generation, or with public utility electricity if the business is operating in a non-Amish industrial park. In some progressive pockets of the Amish world, businesses have signed up for Internet service along with a third-party accountability system and filtering software that sharply limits the Internet to uses such as scheduling shipping or checking a supplier's webpage.

But even within a particular affiliation—including relatively progressive ones—Ordnung regarding technology shifts and changes depending on the social space in which the technology operates, again illustrating that, for the Amish, technology itself is not a problem, but its deployment is carefully monitored. In general the arena with the least technology is the Amish school. A clock, heating stove, and hand pump for water are all the technology most schools

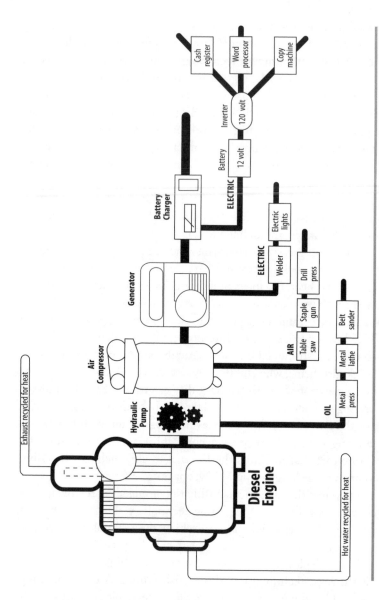

Fig. 7.1. Power Sources Provided by a Diesel Engine

have. There are no calculators, computers, or in most cases indoor plumbing. Schools isolate children from technology and convey the message that technological competency is not that important.

Homes are also devoid of most of the consumer gadgets and communication technologies most Americans take for granted. As the center of family life and the key environment in which children are being raised, homes bear the burden of relatively restrictive Ordnung when it comes to technology. The fact that homes are also the sites of Sunday worship, weddings, and funerals makes them inappropriate places for the intrusive buzzing and beeping that emanates from radios, computers, dishwashers, air conditioners, and other things that produce what most Americans have come to regard as normal background noise. The further one moves away from the home—out into the barn, the shop, or the distant construction site, the looser the restrictions on technology become. For example, many groups that strictly prohibit telephones in the home will allow phones to be installed in shops or in small booths near a shop or barn. The physical location allows the phone to be a work tool and not a device that interrupts meals or encourages long, private conversations.

One of the upshots of the limits that the Amish place on technology is that they have become, in many case, technologically creative and masters of innovation. Because they seek to control technology and not be controlled by it, they are constantly tinkering with things—"Amish-izing" them, as one man put it—to corral technology within the bounds of the Ordnung. The ground-driven power-take-off described at the beginning of this chapter is one of countless inventions and adaptations that have come from self-taught Amish engineers. Some communities have adapted cutting-edge solar power sources. Heavy machinery destined for Amish manufacturing shops is refitted in still other Amish shops by removing the electric motors and other components and replacing them with pneumatic (pressurized air) and hydraulic (pressurized oil) power sources. Over time, the Amish firms specializing in hydraulic work sometimes attract non-Amish clients looking for hydraulic expertise, and then an Amish mechanic finds himself repairing hydraulic components on a dump truck owned by a large non-Amish company down the road.

Creativity, invention, and growth are very often the fruits of restraint.

And although choices about technology reinforce Amish separation from the world, they can also, as the example of the hydraulic shop illustrates, bring the Amish and their neighbors together. Work and technology are but two of the bridges that link the Amish and their neighbors, as we shall see.

CHAPTER EIGHT

The Amish
and Their Neighbors

Stop in Chicago's Union Station on just about any weekday and you'll find Amish families and individuals waiting to switch trains. Although almost all Amish groups permit members to hire drivers to take them on trips that are longer than horse-and-buggy distance, traveling by rail remains a popular option. For members of the most conservative groups, such as the Swartzentruber affiliation that frowns on hiring private drivers, trains and commercial buses are long-distance mainstays.

In 2014 when reporters from Chicago radio station WBEZ decided to do a story on Amish Amtrak riders, they feared the plain-dressed patrons of Union Station would be standoffish. They were delighted instead to discover warm conversationalists, people who enjoyed talking about their trips and even cracked jokes.

Certainly Amish personalities vary, as does the mix of introverts and extroverts in any particular Amish group. But

Amish folks generally are happy to strike up conversations, compare travel notes, or talk about how many grandchildren they have and where those grandchildren live. Swartzentruber families returning to upstate New York from a wedding in Minnesota, for example, arrive home full of stories of the people they met on their cross-country train connections.

For the reporters in Chicago, the Amish in Union Station also provided a snapshot of the many ways Amish people interact with wider society. Some were traveling for business purposes, while a "woman from Ohio was traveling with several of her grandchildren to visit her cousin and see the Grand Canyon." A man from the Midwest was heading to Pennsylvania for a kidney transplant, and another from Kentucky had been in Tijuana, Mexico, where he had gone for surgery because "medical expenses in the States anymore are so phenomenal that an ordinary person cannot afford it."[1]

Commercial connections—which we've seen in the previous chapter—have opened Amish society in many ways. In addition to business, Amish families and individuals find themselves regularly interacting with non-Amish neighbors as members of local civic communities, as they access medical care, and as the subject of a multimillion-dollar Amish-themed tourist industry (chapter 9). Sometimes such interaction centers on legal conflicts or misunderstanding, but for the most part these relationships are marked by generous doses of good will.

Civic Contributions

Most Amish engage their neighbors informally in a wide variety of ways. Contractors may routinely stop at a restaurant for coffee on the way to work and chat with other early morning patrons. Some families develop close friendships with English neighbors and invite them to weddings, funerals, or summer cookouts. In small towns, Amish folks are likely to be on a first-name basis with many business owners, not to mention the drivers they might hire to shuttle them to a distant hospital.

Community engagement through more formal channels varies from location to location. In general, residents of older Amish settlements, where an Amish presence goes back a century or more and relationships have long been woven into the fabric of life, are more apt to engage in civic life than are those living in newer settlements or places where the Amish presence is very small. Amish people do not join service clubs, such as Rotary or Kiwanis, because of their conviction that the church is the only organization in which one should hold any formal membership, but they often support local causes with time and money. In Geauga County, Ohio, for example, Amish people are regular blood donors. In other places Amish households contribute to Habitat for Humanity benefit auctions and make contributions to not-for-profit hospice centers.

There are long-standing connections between the Amish and some volunteer fire companies in Lancaster County, Pennsylvania. Many Amish men participate as firefighters. Although they do not drive the trucks they take part in every other way and receive training in using state-of-the-art firefighting equipment, administering first aid, and conducting search and rescue operations. Crews have sometimes elected an Amish member as the company fire chief. Often self-employed or working in rurally based small shops, Amish men are able to drop everything and respond to a fire call more easily than non-Amish professionals, and some carry small battery-operated beepers.

Amish families have also been central to the funding of Pennsylvania firefighting operations through their donations of time and money to annual fundraising auctions. Popularly known as "mud sales" because they are held in early spring when the ground is thawing, these benefit auctions feature donated goods of all kinds—from housewares and shop tools to books and farm animals—sold by Amish and English auctioneers to crowds of bidders that include every slice of the local community. "It takes everyone working together to make this work," one organizer noted at the 2014 Penryn sale, near the town of Manheim, which attracted more than three thousand people and raised about $20,000 for the North Penryn Fire Company.[2]

Contributions to charity also go global. Amish families back the international aid programs of Mennonite Central Committee (MCC) and Christian Aid Ministries (CAM). Amish volunteers prepare blankets, roll bandages, and can meat for distribution overseas. In a

Amish and non-Amish bidders mingle at an auction held to raise money for the Strasburg Fire Company in Lancaster County, Pennsylvania. Amish men also serve as volunteer firefighters here. *Credit:* Sunday News, *Lancaster, Pa.*

nine-day period in January 2015, for example, Amish men in Goshen, Indiana, processed 78,000 pounds of turkey for shipment via MCC to refugee camps and schools in Africa and Asia. In Kalona, Iowa, Amish volunteers, including young children, gather on weeknights in a CAM warehouse to pack used clothing and sort shoes for worldwide distribution, and three women's sewing circles produce "quilts, comforters, and various other items [that] are sent to the needy" through CAM channels.[3]

Very few Amish people serve internationally with CAM or MCC, but scores of Amish volunteers travel within the United States to assist non-Amish communities each year. Mennonite Disaster Service, an organization somewhat like the Red Cross and headquartered in Lancaster County, Pennsylvania, and Disaster Response Services, a similar agency based in Berlin, Ohio, regularly send busloads of Amish volunteers (and others) to clean up and rebuild homes in the wake of floods, tornadoes, and hurricanes. These groups clocked thousands of hours of Amish labor after Hurricane Katrina struck the Gulf Coast in 2005, for example.

Relations with neighbors are not always smooth. In some communities citizens have complained about horse manure in commercial parking lots or the wear and tear on rural roads from steel-wheeled buggies and metal horseshoes. In 2014 officials in Allen County, Indiana, cited the fact that "about 14 miles of county roads . . . need repair because of damage by horse-drawn vehicles" as reason to increase the county's annual buggy license fee from $30 to $55.[4] In other places a handful of Amish-owned dog breeding businesses have drawn protestors who charge the Amish with operating "puppy mills." Some non-Amish contractors grumble that Amish builders have an unfair advantage because they do not participate in Social Security or, in some states, workers' compensation programs. The fact that the Amish are simply different—that they speak a German dialect, generally do not participate in the public school system or the U.S. military, and seem, in the words of one observer, to be "clannish"—has also soured some people on their Amish neighbors.

Encounters with Government, Politics, and Law

By and large the Amish have not tried to boost their profile politically nor have they sought public influence. Typically they relate to government as subjects rather than as citizens. In other words, their preferred mode of operation is to quietly petition or negotiate for exemptions and special privileges rather than to litigate, lobby, or invoke their constitutional rights. This stance is shaped by Amish values, such as humility, and also by their "two-kingdom" theology that posits a clear distinction between the church and the world. "Graft, corruption, and greed are nearly inseparable from politics," one Amish publication explains, and although the same writer urged readers "to be respectful to the government at all times . . . and pray for our rulers," he is categorical: "Christians have no business in politics."[5]

Nationally, only a small percent of Amish vote on a regular basis, although the rate varies from settlement to settlement, and where the Amish vote they generally cast ballots in local elections rather than state or national contests. In 2004 the Amish in Lancaster, Pennsylvania, received a great deal of media attention when Republican leaders there sought to enlist them—with limited success, it turned out—in President George W. Bush's reelection campaign. "Most of us are armchair Republicans," one man explained, noting that limited government and fiscally and morally conservative rhetoric resonate with his people. However, they do not feel compelled to try and make public policy for everyone. Their sense of faithful "separation from the world" means that they are not driven by a vision of a "Christian America." They seek to respect government but are more inclined to see the state as a necessary evil in a corrupt world rather than something in which they should invest much effort.

Local government, which seems more like a community activity among neighbors, is more apt to draw modest Amish participation. Occasionally they turn out at township meetings at which rural zoning is being debated or they may speak against granting liquor licenses in local villages so as to maintain "dry" communities. Sometimes state or federal legislators will meet with Amish constituents to get their input on legislation that might impinge on Amish practices. This was true in 2009–2010 when the congressman representing eastern Lancaster County worked to ensure that Amish church members would be exempt from portions of the Affordable Care Act.

A group of lay leaders, known as the National Amish Steering Committee, functions as a liaison with government. At a national level, the Steering Committee began in 1966 to negotiate conscientious objection provisions during the Vietnam War–era military draft. Later it broadened its agenda to all sorts of issues, and today there are Steering Committee members active at the state and often local levels across the country, seeking to interact with officials and address open and potential conflicts. The Steering Committee cannot speak definitively for all Amish, but it has smoothed many disagreements—with the Amish often, but not always, getting what they bargain for.

One reason the Amish cannot always speak to government with one voice is that Amish churches themselves do not always agree.

A buggy in the Swartzentruber Amish settlement near Hartshorn, Missouri, does not display an orange slow-moving-vehicle triangle. Members of the highly conservative Swartzentruber affiliation object to the use of the triangles, which has led to conflicts with officials in some states. *Credit: Don Burke*

Highly tradition-minded groups, such as those of the Swartzentruber affiliation, object to affixing bright orange slow-moving-vehicle (S.M.V.) triangles to their buggies. They view the emblems as a pagan talisman that betrays their faith in God's protection on the road. Some states have allowed the Swartzentrubers and other highly conservative affiliations to eschew the S.M.V. triangles, but other states insist on its use. Some of these Amish have spent time in jail for refusing to display the emblem and often have ended up moving to states that are more lenient. Generally, however, Amish welcome the S.M.V. triangles and believe they serve to protect non-Amish drivers from the risk of accidents. They cannot understand the Swartzentrubers' aversion to the triangles and publicly criticize that segment of the Amish world. "It is a privilege and not a right to be on the road," Amish leaders in Bloomfield, Iowa, routinely remind their community, and "a respectful, courteous attitude goes a long way on road safety."[6]

In general, the Amish seek to be law abiding. Amish-perpetrated crime is rare. If an individual is arrested, the default response, drawing on values of Gelassenheit and deference to authority and the practice of confession in church settings, is to waive the right to a lawyer and cooperate with prosecutors. In some cases, church leaders have insisted that Amish defendants not mount a serious defense in court but rather accept whatever sentence is meted out as their punishment for wrongdoing. Court-appointed attorneys for Amish clients have been frustrated with Amish defendants' readiness to confess to whatever the prosecutors throw at them. Plea-bargaining for a lighter sentence strikes many Amish people as dishonest and an exercise in compounding one wrong with another.

When a more abstract legal principle is at stake, such as the free exercise of religion or (in the 1950s and 1960s) the desire of parents to withhold their children from high school, Amish individuals have allowed themselves to be named as plaintiffs in cases being argued by others.

As in any community, some of the most painful Amish legal cases have been those involving domestic or sexual abuse. On the one hand, members of the Amish community have no sympathy for such crimes, which they consider first and foremost profound sin. At the same time, they are often frustrated with or confused by the legal and social services systems that misunderstand or disregard extended family systems, church authority, and the dynamics of community shame when handling such cases. These vibes of distrust, not unlike the distrust toward law enforcement and the judicial system seen in some other minority communities in the United States, can, in turn, be interpreted by criminal justice professionals as Amish disregard for the serious nature of abuse. The result can be a cultural communication impasse that is difficult to bridge.[7]

Health Care and Medicine

With very few exceptions, Amish do not purchase commercial health insurance or participate in public health insurance programs, as described in chapter 4. But that does not mean that they do not engage the health care system, which in the United States is among the most complex social systems. The Amish engage health care on their own terms and mix traditional folkways with modern scientific approaches.

Religious values and convictions shape their understanding of health and medicine. Submission to God's will and a strong belief in life after death mean that, in many cases, Amish people are more apt to accept death as a part of life and not engage in procedures or therapies that prolong the life of a dying person or spend large amounts of money on end-of-life support. As people steeped in the natural world but not schooled in modern science, the Amish are likely to view the purpose of medicine as curing an illness or repairing a broken bone rather than preventing illness or employing invasive therapies. But even in the realm of health care, there is something of a spectrum of Amish practice. Conservative-leaning families, for example, often ignore immunization campaigns, while those on the more change-minded side conscientiously vaccinate their children.

Since no Amish attend college or medical school, there are no Amish doctors, nurses, physical therapists, or other health care professions. In some communities there are Amish women who serve as informal midwives.

Amish communities draw on various resources when facing illness. Folk customs and remedies passed on within families might suggest ways of warding off colds with herbal remedies, for example, or treating minor burns with homemade poultices. In face-to-face communities, knowledge shared among people who have been in similar circumstances is often more plausible than medical advice given by a doctor one does not know and communicated in medical jargon that can easily confuse those with limited formal schooling and for whom English is a second language.

In addition, Amish people tap alternative health care services from non-Amish providers, such as homeopathic treatment, unlicensed midwives, dietary supplements, and the like. The high-touch, low-tech approach of chiropractors and reflexologists make them popular with many Amish people.

Standard health care providers, including hospital emergency rooms and medical doctors and dentists, are also part of the Amish health mix. Most families have a family physician, although the regularity with which they visit the doctor may be less than that of their neighbors, both because Amish families are also drawing on folk and alternative therapies and because many Amish are frugal and view rising health care costs with concern. Nevertheless, it is not uncommon to find Amish patients in the hospital and receiving chemotherapy for cancer, skin grafts following a serious burn, and cataract surgery or hip replacement among the elderly.

Amish-initiated birthing centers and mental health treatment programs illustrate the sort of hybrid approach to care that creatively draws on conventional and alternative health care resources. The Mount Eaton Care Center in Ohio, a childbirth center opened in 1985, offers a birthing environment that combines professional physicians and nursing staff with a low-tech and homey atmosphere that approximates home birth situations. Without having to travel to a more distant hospital obstetrics ward, extended family can more easily visit mothers and babies at Mount Eaton. The professional staff welcomes the involvement of midwives and accepts, without judgment, the non-scientific folk remedies and herbal teas that Amish women believe hasten postpartum recovery. Similar birthing centers have opened in other settlements.

A similar hybrid approach is apparent at Rest Haven, an Amish-conceived and -constructed facility for mental health care that opened in Goshen, Indiana, in 2002. Located on the campus of a professional community mental health center, Rest Haven provides a space for Amish patients to live in a culturally friendly atmosphere devoid of television and other worldly markers. Amish house parents involve patients in meal preparation, lead morning and evening devotions, and welcome visiting family and friends. Patients, meanwhile, have full access to mental health services by walking across the lawn to keep appointments with psychiatrists, psychologists, and counselors.

In the past, some Amish leaders have been wary of mental health professionals, who were seen as promoting an individualistic and highly secular vision of self-fulfillment. Other Amish simply did not share modern psychiatry's understanding of the brain as an organ treatable with drugs or they worried that talk therapy perilously separated thoughts and feelings from soul and spirit. In contrast, Rest Haven has created a trusting relationship among doctors, patients,

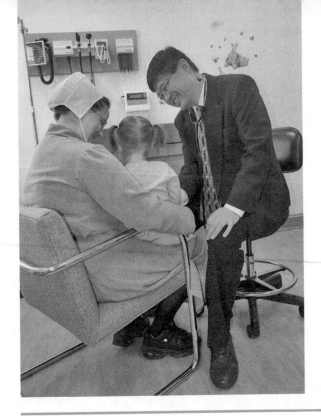

Dr. Heng Wang, an expert in genomic medicine, consults with a patient at the DDC Clinic Center for Special Needs Children in Middlefield, Ohio. The clinic serves more than seven hundred patients from over thirty states and several countries. *Credit: DDC Clinic/Larry Buehner*

and patients' families, and has done a great deal to raise awareness and understanding of mental health issues among the Amish. Its approach and format has been replicated in other places.

Despite their one-armed embrace of modern medicine, Amish people have, perhaps paradoxically, contributed significantly to advancing modern medical knowledge through participation in groundbreaking genetics research. Because of their detailed genealogical records, limited number of immigrant founders, and relatively uniform lifestyle and diet, the Amish are a perfect population for genetic study—a fact that pioneering geneticist Dr. Victor McKusick of Johns Hopkins University School of Medicine recognized in the 1960s when he initiated the first Amish genetics studies. More recently the Clinic for Special Children, directed by Dr. Holmes Morton near Strasburg, Pennsylvania, has been conducting major genetic research with Amish patients, as does the University of Maryland and the DDC Clinic Center for Special Needs Children in Middlefield, Ohio.

Owing to their limited gene pool, the Amish have a higher incidence of some kinds of genetic disorders, for example, limb-girdle muscular dystrophy among the Swiss Amish of Adams County, Indiana. At the same time, a limited gene pool also means that some hereditary disorders are nonexistent in the Amish world. So although the Amish have higher rates of *certain* disorders, they do not necessarily have higher rates of genetic disorder as a whole.

Amish participation in genetic studies has advanced understanding of genomic medicine, heritable diseases, and metabolic disorders. Amish participation in these studies has been remarkable and deeply satisfying to the researchers who work with them. Some Amish have eagerly participated because they know the results may benefit their communities directly, while others participate because they view such work as a way of contributing to the welfare of people everywhere.

Medical research among the Amish also offers the possibility to connect the social and biological components of human health and well-being. For example, an Amish individual with bipolar disorder may be undiagnosed or misdiagnosed because symptoms are culturally bound or culturally expressed in ways that do not match mainstream expectations. Amish studies of the genetic predisposition of bipolar disorder, then, have uncovered issues and questions of culture and diagnosis with implications for the health care of other minority groups.

Cutting-edge genetic studies may not be the first thing that comes to mind when outsiders think of the Amish, but they have become another site of Amish interaction with the modern world. In recent years, those interactions have multiplied and intensified, from tourism to television, with implications for the Amish and the rest of us, alike.

CHAPTER NINE

Amish Images
in Modern America

PUBLISHERS *WEEKLY* LABELED THEM "BONNET RIP-pers"—romance novels with Amish protagonists. With covers featuring young women in plain dress smiling shyly at the reader, the books were a publishing sensation.[1] In 2008 a dozen Amish-themed romance novels hit retail shelves. Two years later there were forty-five releases, and by 2012 publishers were issuing a new Amish romance novel every four days.

Popular interest in the Amish as a people is perhaps nowhere so clear as in the millions of copies of bonnet fiction being snapped up every week in the United States. But just as surely, the mushrooming size of the genre points to the employment and manipulation of the Amish *image* in modern America, an image that says as much—or more—about America as it does about the country's plain people themselves.

On the one hand, the Amish have become remarkably recognizable. Even as Americans tell pollsters they are less sure what distinguishes one religious denomination from another, the Amish stand out more than ever. Everyone from politicians to late night comedians can make reference to the Amish with the confidence that listeners will know whom they are talking about. Without any organized public relations plan, promotional budget, or celebrity spokesperson, a small and self-effacing group has become exceedingly well known. At the same time this recognition, engineered by those outside Amish circles, has transformed them into icons—images through which viewers see something else.

In the case of Amish romance novels, literary critic Valerie Weaver-Zercher has argued that the popularity of these books exposes contemporary readers' weariness of hypersexualized society. Most Amish romance fiction is written and read by evangelical Christians, and the books offer these Americans "chaste texts and chaste protagonists living within a chaste subculture."[2] And although that chaste image comports with Amish values in general, the books rarely stop with an affirmation of Amish religious beliefs. Instead, many of the narratives also critique, at some level, Amish faith and life from an evangelical Christian perspective, often by including characters who leave the Amish world to find personal or religious fulfillment elsewhere or who, at least, entertain those thoughts and thereby affirm the readers' religious sensibilities.

The Amish image in modern America is complicated. And it is a narrative that has been developing for quite some time.

Life in the Public Eye

For much of their history in North America, the Amish attracted scant attention. The Amish were a small group and, if they were noted at all, were lumped with other Pennsylvania German ethnics who were seen as possessing curious customs or peculiar foods. In the early 1930s, for example, restaurant owners in southeastern Pennsylvania who hoped to capitalize on regional cookery sometimes included drawings of Amish people, and occasionally the word "Amish" itself, in cookbooks and menus featuring Pennsylvania German specialties.

The Amish first drew national media attention, however, when their choices pegged them as a people who were not quietly assimilating behind a veneer of distinctive dinner dishes. In 1937 the *New York*

Times ran a series of articles on Amish opposition to a consolidated school building then under construction in East Lampeter Township, Pennsylvania. In the midst of the Great Depression, as communities across the country fought for a share of government money to rebuild aging infrastructure, the Amish rejection of a new building—a building that would spell the end of rural one-room schools—was incomprehensible to journalists. Under headlines such as "Amishmen Battle to Keep Drab Life" reporters described a people who represented the last gasp of unenlightened rural backwardness.[3]

The controversy in East Lampeter fostered a popular perception of the Amish as stubborn people fighting a futile war against progress. In the mid-1900s, as the foreign-born percentage of the U.S. population fell to historic lows, owing to strict immigration laws, academics and civic officials alike were smitten with a national narrative of assimilation and the quiet fading of ethnicity and regionalism. Even the midcentury civil rights movement, which shined a light on minority interests, initially championed social integration rather than cultural differences. In such a context, the image of the Amish as distinctive folk served two related purposes: it affirmed a memory of romantic agrarian independence that harkened back to the nineteenth century, while at the same time reminding the public that progress marched on, despite the dissent of those who were, unfortunately, stuck in the mud.

The Amish way, then, symbolized historic virtues, but virtues that would not be allowed to call into question the country's twentieth-century destiny. The 1955 Broadway production of *Plain and Fancy* presented Amish in such a light. Written by Joseph Stein—later known for *Fiddler on the Roof*, which also traced the decline of traditional communities even as it celebrated their charm—the musical *Plain and Fancy* pictured Amish traditions as needing to give way, sooner or later, to contemporary habits. Lead character Papa Yoder was allowed to criticize some aspects of Cold War America: "Look in your world, and look here! Poor people you have plenty, and worried people and afraid."[4] But in the end, he agreed that Amish ways had no long-term future in the modern world. And why wouldn't he? In a nation pouring millions of dollars into a new interstate highway system and engaged in a space race to place a human on the moon, people who rode in buggies pulled by horses seemed hope-lessly out of touch with the times.

Assuming the Amish were soon to disappear, tour guides and travel promoters scrambled to offer visitors one last glimpse of traditional life before it faded into history. In 1955, the same year the curtain went up on *Plain and Fancy*, the Amish Farm and House opened in Lancaster County, Pennsylvania, as the first paid-admission Amish tourist attraction (the site was not Amish-owned). For East Coast urbanites, especially an older generation who had emigrated from Eastern Europe in the early 1900s, the Amish as an image of a lost peasant past tapped into deep wells of nostalgia.

Then in the 1970s, as an oil embargo, energy crisis, and emerging environmental movement all began to suggest that "small is beauti-ful," the image of Amish as people behind the times was suddenly turned on its head. As a people living off the grid and burning fewer fossil fuels, the Amish suddenly seemed to be a people *ahead* of their time. Amish-themed tourism now shifted gears and turned on the possibility that the Amish might be carriers of cultural wisdom that the rest of the world had discarded in a hurry toward homogeni-zation. At the same time, the revival of mass immigration to the United States was beginning to raise questions about the adequacy of a national assimilationist narrative and the possibility that minor-ity groups, including the Amish, might be here to stay. The 1972 U.S. Supreme Court case legitimating Amish schools was one example of this new narrative of the Amish as a part of pluralistic America.

Meanwhile, a renaissance in folk art, as well as the U.S. bicen-tennial celebration of traditional arts and crafts, suddenly catapulted Amish quilting to prominence. In 1971 the Whitney Museum in New York City included Amish quilts in an exhibit and traveling show of "Abstract Design." Collectors joined tourists flocking to Amish country in search of vibrant tradition. Soon, Doug Tomp-kins, founder of the Esprit clothing line, was hanging Amish quilts throughout his San Francisco office building, moving functional fabric from the bed to the wall and treating it as modern art that was both Americana and avant-garde.

The 1985 Hollywood film *Witness*, starring Harrison Ford and Kelly McGillis, illustrated the new, more celebratory-but-still-

Many Americans nostalgically associate the Amish with an "old-fashioned" way of life. *Credit: Daniel Rodriguez*

uncertain American view of the Amish. They were, on the one hand, commendably different. Just as Americans were beginning to snap up new personal computers, director Peter Weir presented Amish life on the big screen as unplugged, uncluttered, and standing in contrast to the complicated and crime-filled life of a big city detective who ended up hiding out on an Amish farm. Yet, in the end, it was the film's straight-shooting law officer who saved the day. The Amish might be oddly admirable, but they needed to be rescued by Hollywood's redemptive violence as the movie's plot—like Americans in general—did not quite know what to make of them.

An Explosion of Media Images

In the years that followed *Witness*, the Amish image emerged in more and more places, very often as a symbol of wholesome goodness (think "Amish potato salad" at a local deli) but also as a stand-in for naiveté and ignorance. Comedian David Letterman played an outsized role in this development with his inclusion of the Amish among his "Top Ten List" routines, such as "Top Ten Amish Pick-up Lines" (1989) and "Top Ten Amish Spring Break Activities" (1991). Letterman's use of the Amish illustrated the reflexive relationship of mass media stories and popular images, since Letterman's lists often built on current events or nightly news items. For example, his "Top Ten Signs Your Amish Teen Is in Trouble" followed the 1998 story about the arrest of two Amish-reared young men in Pennsylvania as part of a cocaine distribution ring. Earlier, Letterman had helped familiarize audiences with an image of the Amish as too good to be true, an image that made an Amish drug bust story more newsworthy—news that, in turn, provided more comedic material as the Amish seemed to be not very good at all.

In fact, religion and media scholar David Weaver-Zercher has suggested that the Amish image in recent years has actually toggled between *two* images, that of a "saving remnant"—a simple, pious community living life as it once was and still could be—and that of a "fallen people"—the subject of exposés and the butt of jokes purporting to reveal the real and repressed nature of their life.[5]

The relationship between these two images is complex since they rely on one another. For example, *The Devil's Playground*, a 2002 documentary on teenage Amish drug use in northern Indiana, worked only because its racy scenes were coupled with images of quiet pastoralism, naiveté, and utter innocence. Similarly, the chaste theme, on which Amish romance novels capitalize, is easily inverted into an oversexed Amish caricature seen, for example, in the 2008 Hollywood comedy *Sex Drive*. Even when the purpose is purely satire, as in a 2009 story in the online publication *The Onion*—"Amish Woman Knew She Had Quilt Sale the Moment She Laid Eyes on Chicago Couple"—the humor relies on a preexisting image of the Amish as incredibly honest and upstanding.[6] A spate of Amish-themed reality TV shows, from "Amish in the City" (2004) to "Breaking Amish" (2012) to "Amish Mafia" (2012), all worked a similar angle. It mattered little to viewers that the presentation of Rumspringa in the first two series was deeply flawed and that the notion of mafia-style enforcement rings within Amish society was utterly fabricated from start to finish.

Instead, it seems that the conflicting presentations of the Amish as unbelievably good and exceptionally flawed are an expression of a wider phenomenon of contemporary American thinking about difference and diversity. Although multiculturalism has replaced, in many quarters, the language of the melting pot in American cultural discourse, understandings of cultural difference still only go so far. Mainstream faith in assimilation continues to run deep. Differences, many of us seem to believe, exist only on the surface and, in the end, everyone in the United States shares the same hopes, dreams, flaws, and foibles. The message that Amish reality TV shows—and a great many other Amish images in contemporary society—convey is this: even members of a group as striking as the Amish are, deep down, fundamentally no different from the rest of us. We can tolerate them, and other minority groups and interests, not because we are comfortable with difference, but because we are convinced that cultural differences are really just superficial window dressing. In this sense, the Amish image suggests how shallow understandings of multiculturalism and pluralism actually are in the United States today.

Amish Images and Amish Identity

Amish people are not directly responsible for most of the popular images that have flourished around them in the early twenty-first century, but they have not been immune from their impact. As we have seen, Amish identity—like group identity generally—is a negotiated result of characteristics, ascribed and adopted, by outsiders and insiders alike. What others think about the Amish and how they are perceived can open up legal loopholes, create product perception, or curtail economic opportunities. For example, as we've seen, horse-and-buggy transportation becomes a more settled element of Amish identity as non-Amish people come to accept and facilitate it. Store owners put up hitching posts, safety experts design improved lighting and reflectors for buggies, English marketers use carriage logos to label Amish-made products, and non-Amish drivers provide taxi service that allow buggy owners to travel beyond buggy-driving distance.

An Amish woman near Engadine, Michigan, markets quilts to tourists visiting the state's Upper Peninsula to camp and ski. Connections to tourism economies have emerged even in new and more remote settlements. *Credit: Steven Nolt*

Amish involvement with Amish-themed tourism is another example of the church's interaction with popular images. Amish people have often been ambivalent about these encounters, some avoiding them, some complaining about rural roads choked with buses and out-of-state cars, and others actively participating to one degree or another in the tourist trade. Young women work as wait staff in non-Amish-owned restaurants and families sell produce and quilts directly to visitors from home-based shops and roadside stands.

In an essay "Being a Witness to Tourists," an Amish minister, Benuel Blank (1932–2009), reflected on the ways "we plain people can learn a good bit from the very people who would come to see firsthand our way of life and living." For Blank, the attention that his church attracted raised the bar for his people's behavior. Others *expect* to see Amish simplicity, and Blank believed his people were more than obligated to deliver. "Since our way of living is being so closely watched and studied," he told his Amish readers, "we are more responsible than ever for the way we live." After all, "our lives are the only Bible that many [tourists] may ever 'read.'" As he reflected on his interactions over the years with tourists sporting ever-changing fashion, Blank found himself "thankful for our church ordnung in clothing" since "with our ordnung we do not have to get a complete new set of clothes every time the styles and fashions of the world change." Thus, scrutiny from outside prompted him to "try to help keep our way of life from becoming even more materialistic than it is now."[7]

Benuel Blank's ruminations point to the dynamic character of Amish culture. No culture is static, nor is change a one-way street. Some Amish groups have become more technologically conservative over time, for example, and parents in some settlements have trumped tradition by restricting or redirecting Rumspringa activities. The Amish have never been isolated from the currents of modernity. Amish business owners, for example, understand the commercial logic of economies of scale and some hear the authoritative voice of efficiency. In an essay on "wasted motion," for example, one shop owner offered a remarkably rational analysis of production. Assuming a woodworking shop had eight employees and each took several more seconds than absolutely necessary to move from one step of a task to another, he calculated that production would decline and income would plunge $5,760 a year. "If you avoid needless moves," he concluded, "your profits will increase."[8] The shifting edges of acceptable behavior and the presence of certain modern modes of thought and action—prizing efficiency, appreciating growth, thinking strategically—are part of what it means to negotiate the Amish way in the contemporary world.

A Model Minority?

What does all the attention the Amish garner, as well as their dynamic group identity, say about the contours of contemporary multicultural America? In some ways the Amish are a unique minority, but in other ways their experience is akin to that of other distinctive subcultures that thrive—despite being misunderstood—in pluralistic America.

The Amish might be considered a model minority. They have successfully negotiated a comfortable place in the United States, enjoying the benefits of religious liberty and the affection of many outsiders who buy their goods, crave their quilts, and see in them the sturdy values of honesty and good hard work. Stubborn resistance and patient negotiation—sometimes literal, sometimes metaphorical—has resulted in a range of legal exemptions from high school attendance and Social Security payroll taxes to provisions of the Affordable Care Act and more. Meanwhile, Amish goods generally benefit from positive brand association and a public perception that "Amish-made" equals quality and value. Amish folks recognize the generally positive public perception they enjoy, and they worry about it. After all, they remind one another, Jesus said, "Woe unto you, when all men shall speak well of you" (Luke 6:26).

Certainly the Amish have benefitted from the principle of freedom of religion enshrined in the U.S. Constitution and the civil rights revolution that has slowly extended legal protection to a wider array of people and groups. Undoubtedly the Amish have also benefitted from America's generally positive view of "colorful" white minorities, as opposed to its minorities of color. The fact that the Amish embrace private property, ask relatively little of larger society, do not proselytize, and reside in rural areas that are often ignored by public policy makers also contributes to their benign image.

To be sure, Amish people have not always been the subjects of adulation. Especially in wartime, and as German-speakers, their peace convictions were unpopular. Some sat in jail as religious liberty cases brought on their behalf wound their way through the courts. And an undercurrent of anti-Amish bias is part of the public discourse in many places, whether because neighbors believe the Amish are not shouldering their fair share of civic responsibility or because the plain people simply seem standoffish and different.

Yet, on the whole, the Amish have been remarkably successful dissenters. As the preceding chapters have argued, the Amish are not simply people who dress oddly but are otherwise "just like the

Amish and English families play together at a public park. Many Amish enjoy neighborly friendships while still standing apart from the North American mainstream. *Credit: Dottie Kauffmann/Mennonite Historical Library*

rest of us." Rather, they resist, actively, the forces of assimilation that come from public education, retain a German dialect as their mother tongue, dissent from displays of patriotism, and they refuse, on the whole, to accept that the individual is the unit of analysis and measure of success when it comes to gauging human fulfillment. They believe that limits are essential to happiness rather than barriers to achieving fulfillment. The animating values of Amish life and culture stand in sharp contrast to key American myths and cultural assumptions.

And yet the Amish have a way of unsettling us. They thrive in the midst of modern society. They are not going away and, in fact, are growing and establishing new communities each year. But it is more than just their growth that disquiets the rest of us. The Amish are committed to values that run counter to deeply held American commitments. They limit education, revere tradition, and stifle individual accomplishment. Commentators from wider society are often at pains to show that the Amish are hypocritical or inconsistent, as if establishing that fact could dismiss the alternative example the Amish way poses.

Yet if popular images of the Amish are really more about us than them—more about modern hopes and fears than about actual Amish concerns—then the question of why the Amish hold our gaze is actually a question of whether the myths and values that animate modern life are the only keys to human flourishing. The Amish embrace limits and they have decided that exchanging much individual choice for a sense of collective purpose and security is a healthy bargain. Few of us in the wider world would consider making that exchange on the terms the Amish have set. But in a postmodern society marked by anomie, avatars, and artificial reality, the Amish raise the question of where in our world authentic and meaningful choices lie. Asking such questions does not mean that the rest of us will or want to become Amish. But by noticing their choices, the rest of us may recognize more clearly our own deepest assumptions. Doing so may lead us to question or temper those assumptions. Or it may allow us to embrace our own values more consciously and willingly rather than thoughtlessly or haphazardly.

If so, the Amish will have served the rest of us well, even as they pursue their own ends for their own reasons.

APPENDIX A: Amish Spirituality
Excerpts from Rules of a Godly Life

The following excerpts from "Rules of a Godly Life" ("Regeln eines Gottseli-gen Lebens") provide something of the flavor of Amish spirituality. "Rules" has long been a popular devotional source among the Amish, although it was not penned by an Amish writer. Its origin is obscure, but the earliest known edition appeared in 1736 and since then has often been included in prayer books compiled by the Amish. The translation here was done by an Ontario Amish minister and appears in its entirety in *In Meiner Jugend: A Devotional Reader in German and English* (Aylmer, Ont.: Pathway Publishers, 2000), 65–103.

Rules of a Godly Life

In the morning, awake with God and consider that this might be your final day. When you go to bed at night, you do not know if you will ever rise again, except to appear before the Judgment. For this reason, it is all the more expedient for you to pray every day, falling upon your knees both mornings and evenings, confessing your sins to God and asking His forgiveness, and thanking Him for blessings received. . . .

If anyone wrongs you, bear it patiently. For if you take the wrong to heart or become angry, you hurt no one but yourself and are only doing what your enemy would like for you to do, giving him the satisfaction of seeing how annoyed you are. But if you can be patient, God will in His good time judge rightly and bring your innocence to light. . . .

If other people praise you for some virtue, humble yourself. But do not praise yourself, for that is the way of fools who seek vain glory. In all your dealings be honest—that will be reward enough and others will praise you. . . .

In suffering be patient, and silence your heart under the mighty hand of God with these meditations: first, that it is God's hand that chastens you; second, that it is for your benefit; third, that He will ease the burden; fourth, He will give you strength to endure; and fifth, He will deliver you from affliction in due time. . . .

Think that for every idle word you speak you must give account thereof in the day of judgment (Matthew 12:36). "In the multitude of words, there wanteth not sin" (Proverbs 10:19). So try to avoid idle talk and let your speech be deliberate, of few words, and truthful. Consider beforehand if what you are about to say is worth saying. Practice saying much in few words. Never state anything as true and authentic if you do not know for certain that it is so, and rather remain silent than to say something which may be false or otherwise of no value. . . .

Do not make fun of another's weaknesses, but think of your own shortcomings (Galatians 6). We all have our faults and there is no one of whom it is not said, "Oh, if only this were not!" Either we are, or have been, or can become what another is. For this reason, have patience and sympathy with your neighbor's weakness and frailty. . . .

Everyone most certainly needs correction at times. For as the eye sees all and seeks the improvement of all yet cannot see itself or better itself, so by our very natures we are partial to ourselves and cannot see our own shortcomings and defects as easily as we can see those of other people. For this reason it is very needful that our faults be pointed out to us—which others can see so much more clearly than we ourselves can see them. . . .

Resist with all strength of soul your bosom sin, or that sin to which your nature is inclined more than to all other sins. For one person this may be to seek the honor of men, for another a greed for money, a third may tend to drunkenness, a fourth to impurity, a fifth to pride. Against these evil sins you must above all arm yourself and resist them, for once these are overcome you can also easily master others. As a fowler can hold a bird by one leg, in the same way wily Satan can possess your soul and keep it in his control by means of a single sin just as well as by many. . . .

Strive to be an upright servant of Jesus Christ, not only outwardly in public services to hear God's Word and the religious observances of the Gospel, but also in your whole life by renouncing all sin and in true obedience to live according to all the commandments of God. Do not be satisfied when others think of you as being devout—but truly be in reality what you appear to be. Woe to the man who is not pious yet wants to be considered as such. . . .

Avoid idleness as a resting-pillow of the devil and a cause of all sorts of wickedness. Be diligent in your calling so that the devil never finds you idle. Great is the power the devil has over the slothful, to plunge them into all kinds of sins, for idleness gives rise to every vice. It was when David was idle on his housetop that he became an adulterer (2 Samuel 11:2–5). . . .

Strive at all times to be respectable in your clothes and have nothing to do with the vexing pomp and display of raiment. It is a great vanity to spend as much on one suit as would clothe two or three persons. If you in your old age were to think back to how much time you spent merely to adorn yourself, you could not but grieve that you ever loved such vain display.

Read often in God's Word, and you will find many warnings against pride. You will see that no sin was punished more severely than pride. It changed angels into devils, and the powerful King Nebuchadnezzar into a wild beast. It was because of pride that Jezebel was eaten by dogs (2 Kings 9:30–37). . . .

No one is his own master, only a steward over that which he has and possesses. Therefore, you must distribute of your goods to the needy, and do it wisely, willingly, and from the heart (Romans 21:13; 2 Corinthians 9:7). . . .

Finally, in your conduct be friendly toward everyone and a burden to none. Toward God, live a holy life; toward yourself, be moderate; toward your fellow men, be fair; in life, be modest; in your manner, courteous; in admonition, friendly; in forgiveness, willing; in your promises, true; in your speech, wise; and out of a pure heart gladly share of the bounties you receive.

Appendix B: Related Groups
Mennonites, Beachy Amish, Hutterites

The Amish are perhaps the best known of groups that descend from the Anabaptist movement of the sixteenth century (chapter 2), but they are not alone. *Mennonite* churches in North America today roughly fall into two types: traditional and assimilated. Members of assimilated churches, such as Mennonite Church USA and the Mennonite Brethren, participate in many aspects of mainstream culture. They pursue higher education, live in urban areas, engage in professions, use up-to-date technology, and wear contemporary clothing.

Plain-dressing, traditional Mennonites include horse-and-buggy-driving *Old Order Mennonites*. Like the Amish, Old Order Mennonites emerged in the later 1800s and shared many of the same critiques of industrializing society. They have also continued to speak Pennsylvania Dutch. Several customs distinguish the two groups. For example, unlike the Amish, the Old Order Mennonite men do not have beards, and the fabrics worn by Old Order Mennonite women typically have patterns and designs in contrast to the solid fabrics of Amish women. Old Order Mennonites worship in simple church meetinghouses, unlike the Amish, who meet for worship in private homes.

Other traditional Mennonites, including the Wisler Mennonites and the Weaverland Mennonites, drive cars. They wear plain dress and rarely attend college. They use electricity but limit television and online access.

The *Beachy Amish* and the so-called *Amish-Mennonites* are groups that emerged in the twentieth century from Amish roots. Despite their names and history, these churches lie outside the contemporary Amish orbit because their members drive cars and use a wide range of consumer technology and few speak Pennsylvania Dutch. These groups typically engage in vigorous evangelism and mission work and have gained many converts of non-Amish background. Male members have closely trimmed beards and women wear small head coverings. Some members pursue higher education.

The *Hutterites*, who practice economic communalism, branched from the Anabaptist movement in 1528 in Europe. They reject private property and base their communalism on practices of the early Christian church. More than fifty thousand Hutterites live in rural communes in the northern plains states and in western Canada. They wear distinctive garb and speak a German dialect. Unlike the Amish, however, they use the most advanced farm technology and motor vehicles, all of which are communally owned.

Several other groups are easily confused with the Amish. The *Old German Baptist Brethren* and the *Old Order River Brethren* are often misidentified as Amish because their distinctive clothing resembles Amish dress and because Brethren men also grow full beards. However, members of these Brethren groups drive cars, use electricity, and permit higher education and use of the Internet. They do not speak a German dialect. Brethren churches trace their history both to the Anabaptist movement of the 1500s and to a 1600s renewal movement known as Pietism.

Four other groups are sometimes mistakenly associated with the Amish: the *Quakers*, the *Amana Colonies*, the *Moravians*, and the *Shakers*. None of these groups has direct historical or religious connections to the Amish. Several of these groups, at least in their past, have had some practices—pacifism, plain dress, separation from the larger society—that resemble Amish ways and have led to the understandable confusion.

For more detail, see Donald B. Kraybill. *Concise Encyclopedia of Amish, Brethren, Hutterites, and Mennonites*. Baltimore: Johns Hopkins University Press, 2010.

Notes

Chapter 1. Meet the Amish

1. *Die Botschaft*, April 15, 2013, 80.

2. The bargaining metaphor is expanded in Donald B. Kraybill, Karen M. Johnson-Weiner, and Steven M. Nolt, *The Amish* (Baltimore: Johns Hopkins University Press, 2013), and Donald B. Kraybill, *The Riddle of Amish Culture*, rev. ed. (Baltimore: Johns Hopkins University Press, 2001).

3. Amish Studies website provides annually updated data on Amish population by state. http://www2.etown.edu/amishstudies/Index.asp.

Chapter 2. Amish Roots

1. The literature on the Reformation is, of course, immense, and the few lines here emphasize an interpretation which the Amish espouse. For a general overview, and one that is less sectarian, see C. Scott Dixon, *Contesting the Reformation* (Walden, Mass.: Wiley-Blackwell, 2012).

2. *Songs of the* Ausbund: *History and Translation of* Ausbund *Hymns*, vol. 1 (Millersburg, Ohio: Ohio Amish Library, 1998), 347–53. This translation was made by a committee of Amish historians. The story of Hans Haslibacher is also included in *Martyrs Mirror*.

3. See chapter 2 in Steven M. Nolt, *A History of the Amish*, 3rd ed. (New York: Good Books, 2015); primary sources are available in English as John D. Roth, trans. and ed., *Letters of the Amish Division: A Source Book* (Goshen, Ind.: Mennonite Historical Society, 1993).

4. John Hüppi, "Research Note: Identifying Jacob Ammann," *Mennonite Quarterly Review* 74 (April 2000): 332.

5. Ammann was likely building on a wider Anabaptist renewal movement that included other Swiss preachers. Leroy Beachy, *Unser Leit: The Story of the Amish* (Millersburg, Ohio: Goodly Heritage Books, 2011), 35–110, gives Ulrich Muller a prominent place in the narrative of Amish origins; most scholarly assessments see Ammann as the key figure in the formation of the Amish as a distinct group in the 1690s.

6. The Dortrecht Confession is available at http://en.wikisource.org/wiki/Dordrecht_Confession_of_Faith.

7. Roth, *Letters*, 24, 118.

8. Robert Baecher, "Research Note: The 'Patriarche' of Sainte-Marie-aux-Mines," *Mennonite Quarterly Review* 74 (Jan. 2000): 151–52.

9. Ibid., 152–54.

10. Robert Baecher, "1712: Investigation of an Important Date," trans. by Kevin J. Ruth, *Pennsylvania Mennonite Heritage* 21 (April 1998): 6.

11. What happened to Ammann himself after 1712 is unclear. It seems he had died by 1730.

12. Nolt, *A History of the Amish*, 72–84, 122–33.

13. For more discussion, see chapter 6 in Nolt, *A History of the Amish*.

14. John S. Umble, trans. and ed., "Memoirs of an Amish Bishop," *Mennonite Quarterly Review* 22 (April 1948): 101–4.

15. Leroy Beachy, trans., "Old Set of Rules—Orderly Church Conduct," *Plain Interests* (January 2013): 5.

16. The Mennonites who absorbed the change-minded Amish were the branches more open to adapting to their North American environment, building denominational institutions, pursuing higher education, and so on. There were a number of Mennonite groups in North America, including a traditionalist Old Order Mennonite branch that was similar to the Old Order Amish in several ways. See appendix B.

17. "Charles F. Richter: How It Was," *Engineering and Science* 45, no. 4 (March 1982): 24–28. Richter's birth name was Charles Kinsinger (a common Amish surname), but soon after he moved to southern California as a boy with his maternal grandfather Richter, he adopted that grandfather's surname.

18. Donald B. Kraybill, ed., *The Amish and the State*, 2nd ed. (Baltimore: Johns Hopkins University Press, 2003).

Chapter 3. Living the Old Order

1. James T. Patterson, *Grand Expectations: The United States, 1945–1974* (New York: Oxford University Press, 1996), 281–82.

2. Sprint "I am unlimited" advertisement, 2013, available at https://youtube/GCUO3-yq3eg.

3. Connections between technology, efficiency, segmentation, modernity, and culture have been explored by many scholars and thoughtful journalists, including Howard Gardner and Katie Davis, *The App Generation: How Today's Youth Navigate Identity, Intimacy, and Imagination in a Digital World* (New Haven, Conn.: Yale University Press, 2013); Sherry Turkle, *Alone Together: Why We Expect*

More from Technology and Less from Each Other (New York: Basic Books, 2011); Barry Schwartz, *The Paradox of Choice: Why More Is Less* (New York: Ecco, 2004); and Nicholas Carr, *The Shallows: What the Internet Is Doing to Our Brains* (New York: W. W. Norton, 2010).

4. The word *Gelassenheit* is not common in Amish speech because it is a High German, rather than Pennsylvania Dutch, term. But the word accurately sums up central Amish values. The term is not entirely absent from Amish discourse; see a twenty-first century example in Paul Kline (below). Bishop David Beiler, a leading nineteenth-century Old Order Amish writer, used the term Gelassenheit to describe Jesus's character that should be imitated; see Beiler, *Das Wahre Christenthum: Eine Christliche Betrachtung nach der Heiligen Schrift* (Lancaster, Pa.: Johann Bär's Söhnen, 1888), 129.

5. Paul Kline, "Gelassenheit," unpublished notes, Holmes County, Ohio, n.d., author's files.

6. Ibid.

7. *1001 Questions and Answers on the Christian Life* (Aylmer, Ont.: Pathway Publishers, 1992), 141–42.

8. J.F.B. [Joseph F. Beiler], "Research Note: Ordnung," *Mennonite Quarterly Review* 56 (October 1982): 383–84.

9. There are a few cases in which aspects of Ordnung might be written down. If a new Amish settlement is formed by people from different communities of origin with different understandings of Ordnung, some potentially contentious points might be reduced to print to make sure everyone shares the same working assumptions.

10. For discussion of these and other Amish subgroups, see chapter 8 in Donald B. Kraybill, Karen M. Johnson-Weiner, and Steven M. Nolt, *The Amish* (Baltimore: Johns Hopkins University Press, 2013).

Chapter 4. Community and Church

1. Harvey Yoder, "Remembering My Amish Baptism," *Mennonite World Review*, July 11, 2014, available at http://mennoworld.org/2014/07/11/the-world -together/remembering-my-amish-baptism-60-years-later/.

2. Steven M. Nolt, "Inscribing Community: *The Budget* and *Die Botschaft* in Amish Life," 181–98, in *The Amish and the Media*, ed. Diane Zimmerman Umble and David L. Weaver-Zercher (Baltimore: Johns Hopkins University Press, 2008). *The Budget* is published by a non-Amish publisher in Sugarcreek, Ohio. The description here is of the "National Edition" of *The Budget*, which is an Amish correspondence paper. The publisher also issues a "Local Edition," also titled *The Budget*, for residents of the town of Sugarcreek; that paper is a conventional newspaper with headlines, photos, and so on. *Die Botschaft*

is published in Millersburg, Pennsylvania, and today has an Amish publisher.

3. For more detail on Amish religious life and spirituality, see Donald B. Kraybill, Steven M. Nolt, and David L. Weaver-Zercher, *The Amish Way: Patient Faith in a Perilous World* (San Francisco: Jossey-Bass, 2010).

4. "Church Services in the Home," *Family Life*, June 2013, 11.

5. Ibid.

6. Data on retention rates in various communities are reported in Donald B. Kraybill, Karen M. Johnson-Weiner, and Steven M. Nolt, *The Amish* (Baltimore: Johns Hopkins University Press, 2013), 162–68.

Chapter 5. *Rumspringa*: Amish Gone Wild?

1. Gil Smart, "Hitchin' Up Buggy and . . . Facebook," *Lancaster Sunday News*, June 19, 2011, A-1. Richard A. Stevick's comprehensive study, *Growing Up Amish: The Rumspringa Years*, 2nd ed. (Baltimore: Johns Hopkins University Press, 2014), includes results of his study of Amish social media use; see esp. pp. 124, 139, 142, 150, 178, 189, and 201–7.

2. Bart Yassos, "Running with the Amish," *Runners World*, March 2012, 92–102.

3. Stevick, *Growing Up Amish*, 228.

Chapter 6. Family and Schooling

1. Loren Beachy, "The Plain Side: A Hearty Parlor Tussle with Pictionary," *Goshen News*, April 19, 2014, A-3; http://www.goshennews.com/lifestyles /x2117339809/PLAIN-SIDE-A-hearty-parlor-tussle-with-Pictionary.

2. Almost every family also has one or more English-language King James translations of the Bible. About 6 percent of the total Amish population descends from a cohort of Amish immigrants who came from Switzerland in the 1850s and settled in certain pockets in the Midwest. These Amish speak a distinctive Swiss-German dialect that Pennsylvania Dutch–speaking Amish find hard to decipher.

3. *Marriage Meeting, October 20 & 27, 2007* (Dundee, Ohio: Family Helpers, n.d.), 37.

4. Sam S. Stoltzfus, "Our Plain Folks and Their Spirituality," *The Connection: Connecting Our Amish Communities*, August 2009, 55.

5. Ibid.

6. Joseph Stoll, *Who Shall Educate Our Children?* (Aylmer, Ont.: Pathway Publishing, 1965), 23.

7. *Indiana Amish Directory: Elkhart, LaGrange, and Noble Counties, 2012* (Middlebury, Ind.: Jerry E. Miller, 2012), 13.

8. Quoted in Donald B. Kraybill, *The Riddle of Amish Culture*, rev. ed. (Baltimore: Johns Hopkins University Press, 2001), 162.

9. Donald B. Kraybill, Karen M. Johnson-Weiner, and Steven M. Nolt, *The Amish* (Baltimore: Johns Hopkins University Press, 2013), 263–64.

Chapter 7. Work and Technology

1. All quotations in this section are from *Horse Progress Days: Something for Everyone, 20th Annual Event*, July 5–6, 2013, program book, 165 pages. The 2015 program booklet, *22nd Annual Horse Progress Days*, July 3–4, Daviess County, Indiana, includes several essays on the event's origins.

2. *1001 Questions and Answers on the Christian Life* (Aylmer, Ont.: Pathway Publishers, 1992), 138–39.

3. Randall E. James, "Horse and Human Labor Estimates for Amish Farms," *Journal of Extension*, 45, no. 1 (February 2007), at http://www.joe.org/joe/2007february/rb5.php.

4. Jerry L. Miller, "Change to Organic Farming," *Family Life* (January 2007), 34.

5. Many of the observations that follow are detailed in Donald B. Kraybill and Steven M. Nolt, *Amish Enterprise: From Plows to Profits*, 2nd ed. (Baltimore: Johns Hopkins University Press, 2004).

Chapter 8. The Amish and Their Neighbors

1. Katie Klocksin, "Passing Through: Chicago's Union Station as Amish Transit Hub," *Curious City*, a production of WBEZ Chicago, July 7, 2014; archived at http://www.wbez.org/series/curious-city/passing-through-chicagos-union-station-amish-transit-hub-110453.

2. David O'Connor, "Thousands Flock to Penryn for Annual Mud Sale," Lancaster Online, March 15, 2014, http://lancasteronline.com/news/local/thousands-flock-to-penryn-for-annual-mud-sale/article_f8a26d24-ac6e-11e3-9d63-0017a43b2370.html.

3. J. Tyler Klassen, "MCC Mobile Canner Provides Food Relief around the World," *Elkhart Truth*, Jan. 11, 2015, p. 1; *Iowa Amish Directory, 2004* (Millersburg, Ohio: Abana Books, 2004), 159.

4. Dan Stockman, "Buggy License Fees Shoot Up; County Cites Heavy Cost of Road Repair," [Fort Wayne, Ind.] *Journal Gazette*, February 22, 2014; http://www.journalgazette.net/article/20140222/LOCAL/302229982.

5. *1001 Questions and Answers on the Christian Life* (Aylmer, Ont: Pathway Publishers, 1992), 157–59.

6. "Bloomfield Safety Committee Meeting," *The Grapevine*, 9, no. 2 (Jan. 15, 2014), 10.

7. See James A. Cates, *Serving the Amish: A Cultural Guide for Professionals* (Baltimore: Johns Hopkins University Press, 2014), for an excellent introduction to constructive approaches to these and other issues.

Chapter 9. Amish Images in Modern America

1. "Romancing the Recession," *Publishers Weekly*, November 16, 2009, accessed at http://www.publishersweekly.com/pw/print/20091116/28360-romancing-the -recession.html.

2. Valerie Weaver-Zercher, *Thrill of the Chaste: The Allure of Amish Romance Novels* (Baltimore: Johns Hopkins University Press, 2013), 13.

3. *New York Times*, August 15, 1937, 36.

4. Joseph Stein and Will Glickman, *Plain and Fancy: A Musical Comedy* (New York: Random House, 1955), 91.

5. David L. Weaver-Zercher, *The Amish in the American Imagination* (Baltimore: Johns Hopkins University Press, 2001), 185–96. Other sources that have informed this chapter are Janneken Smucker, *Amish Quilts: Crafting an American Icon* (Baltimore: Johns Hopkins University Press, 2013); Susan L. Trollinger, *Selling the Amish: The Tourism of Nostalgia* (Baltimore: Johns Hopkins University Press, 2012); and Thomas J. Meyers, "Amish Tourism: 'Visiting Shipshewana Is Better Than Going to the Mall,'" *Mennonite Quarterly Review* 77 (January 2003): 109–26.

6. http://www.theonion.com/articles/amish-woman-knew-she-had-quilt -sale-the-moment-she,6888/.

7. Benuel Blank, "Being a Witness to Tourists," 151–56, in *The Scriptures Have the Answers: Inspirational Writings by Ben Blank* (Parksburg, Pa.: The Blank Family, 2009).

8. Moses B. Glick, "Shopworker's Diary," *The Diary*, June 1993, 38.

For Further Reading

Comprehensive Study of Amish Life

Kraybill, Donald B., Karen M. Johnson-Weiner, and Steven M. Nolt. *The Amish*. Baltimore: Johns Hopkins University Press, 2013.

Contemporary Amish Life

Johnson-Weiner, Karen M. *Train Up a Child: Old Order Amish and Mennonite Schools*. Baltimore: Johns Hopkins University Press, 2006.
 Curricula, parent-teacher interaction, and philosophy of education, with attention to how schools not only shape but also reflect their particular settlements.

Kraybill, Donald B. *The Amish and the State*. 2nd ed. Baltimore: Johns Hopkins University Press, 2003.
 Chapters on topics such as Social Security, health care, slow-moving-vehicle issues, land use, and the role of outsiders in legal negotiation.

Kraybill, Donald B., and Steven M. Nolt. *Amish Enterprise: From Plows to Profits*. 2nd ed. Baltimore: Johns Hopkins University Press, 2004.
 A look at the shift from farming to small business entrepreneurship and the implications for Amish society.

Louden, Mark L. *Pennsylvania Dutch: The Story of an American Language*. Baltimore: Johns Hopkins University Press, 2015.
 A close look at the place of the language in the life and culture of the Amish, as well as non-Amish, speakers of this oral vernacular.

Stevick, Richard A. *Growing Up Amish: The Rumspringa Years*. Rev. ed. Baltimore: Johns Hopkins University Press, 2014.
 Amish youth culture, courtship, and marriage by an educational psychologist.

Religion and Spirituality

Elder, D. Rose. *Why the Amish Sing: Songs of Solidarity and Identity*. Baltimore: Johns Hopkins University Press, 2014.
 How music functions in church, home, school, and community, written by an ethnomusicologist.

Kraybill, Donald B., Steven M. Nolt, and David Weaver-Zercher. *Amish Grace: How Forgiveness Transcended Tragedy*. San Francisco: Jossey-Bass, 2007. Examines Amish understandings of forgiveness in the aftermath of the 2006 Nickel Mines Amish school shooting.

Kraybill, Donald B., Steven M. Nolt, and David Weaver-Zercher. *The Amish Way: Patient Faith in a Perilous World*. San Francisco: Jossey-Bass, 2010. Exploration of Amish spirituality and religious practices.

History

Nolt, Steven M. *A History of the Amish*. 3rd ed. New York: Good Books, 2015. Overview of Amish history in Europe and North America from the 1690s to the present.

Roth, John D., trans. and ed. *Letters of the Amish Division: A Sourcebook*. Goshen, Ind.: Mennonite Historical Society, 1993. Documents from 1693 to 1720 detailing debates surrounding the origins of the Amish, including writings of Jakob Ammann.

Studies of Specific Settlements

Hurst, Charles E., and David L. McConnell. *An Amish Paradox: Diversity and Change in the World's Largest Amish Community*. Baltimore: John Hopkins University Press, 2010. Detailed look at the Holmes-Wayne Counties, Ohio, settlement, with special attention to issues of family, schooling, work, and health care.

Johnson-Weiner, Karen M. *New York Amish: Life in the Plain Communities of the Empire State*. Ithaca, N.Y.: Cornell University Press, 2010. A comparison of five quite different Amish settlements, from highly traditional to more progressive.

Kraybill, Donald B. *The Riddle of Amish Culture*. Rev. ed. Baltimore: Johns Hopkins University Press, 2001. Classic study of social change in the Lancaster, Pennsylvania, settlement, including issues of technology, schooling, and the social structure of the community.

Nolt, Steven M., and Thomas J. Meyers. *Plain Diversity: Amish Cultures and Identities*. Baltimore: Johns Hopkins University Press, 2007. A comparison of nineteen Amish settlements in Indiana, analyzed through the lenses of migration, ethnicity, economic contexts, and church Ordnung.

The Amish and the Rest of Us

Cates, James A. *Serving the Amish: A Cultural Guide for Professionals.* Baltimore: Johns Hopkins University Press, 2014.

Written for medical staff, law enforcement, social workers, and counselors who work with Amish clients, by a board-certified clinical psychologist.

Trollinger, Susan L. *Selling the Amish: The Tourism of Nostalgia.* Baltimore: Johns Hopkins University Press, 2012.

Examines tourism in four towns in Holmes County, Ohio, and surrounding area.

Umble, Diane Zimmerman, and David L. Weaver-Zercher, eds. *The Amish and the Media.* Baltimore: Johns Hopkins University Press, 2008.

Essays on journalism, television, feature and documentary films, as well as Amish-produced publications.

Weaver-Zercher, David. *The Amish in the American Imagination.* Baltimore: Johns Hopkins University Press, 2001.

Analyzes popular representations of the Amish in tourism, novels, Broadway, and Hollywood, and asks what those views say about American culture.

Weaver-Zercher, Valerie. *Thrill of the Chaste: The Allure of Amish Romance Novels.* Baltimore: Johns Hopkins University Press, 2013.

Explores the phenomenon of Amish-themed romance fiction from the perspective of writers, publishers, booksellers, and readers—including Amish readers.

Amish-Authored or -Issued Works

1001 Questions and Answers on the Christian Life. Aylmer, Ont.: Pathway Publishers, 1992.

Amish-authored explanations of key beliefs and practices, with biblical references.

Ausbund: Das ist, Etliche schöne Christliche Lieder. Lancaster, Pa.: The Amish Book Committee, 1996.

Hymnal used by the Amish in worship. Contains 140 hymn texts from the sixteenth and seventeenth centuries.

Braght, Thieleman J. van, comp. *The Bloody Theater or Martyrs Mirror of the Defenseless Christians.* 2nd English ed., 24th printing. Scottdale, Pa.: Herald Press, 2002.

Anabaptist church history book, first published in Dutch in 1660. This English edition, or an Amish-published German edition, is common in Amish homes.

A Devoted Christian's Prayer Book. Aylmer, Ont.: Pathway Publishers, 1995.
   English translation of a 1739 Anabaptist devotional book, *Die Ernsthafte
   Christenpflicht*, containing prayers for all occasions, frequently used by the
   Amish.
Family Life. Alymer, Ont: Pathway Publishers.
   A monthly family and community magazine, issued by an Amish
   publisher with articles by Amish and Old Order Mennonite writers.
In Meiner Jugend: A Devotional Reader in German and English. Translated by
   Joseph Stoll. Aylmer, Ont.: Pathway Publishers, 2000.
   Prayers, devotional readings, and texts used in baptisms and weddings,
   plus the Dordrecht Confession of Faith and Rules of a Godly Life.

Digital Resources

The Amish. Produced by David Belton. Boston: American Experience Films/
   Sarah Colt Productions, 2012. DVD.
   A 120-minute documentary exploring the beliefs, lifestyle, and history of
   the Amish, as well as their complex relationship to mainstream American
   culture.
Amish Studies website: http://www2.etown.edu/amishstudies/
   Reliable information on Amish life and culture, developed by the Young
   Center for Anabaptist and Pietist Studies at Elizabethtown College.

Index

abuse, 52, 62, 71, 102

acceptance. See *Gelassenheit*

Adams County, Indiana, 106

adaptation, 7–9, 35–36; and technology, 33–34, 80–81, 93

adolescence, 49, 53–61; and deviant behavior, 58–60; and identity, 56–58; and peer groups, 54–55, 57–61

affiliations, 37–39, 64, 76, 79, 91

Affordable Care Act, Patient Protection and (2010), 100, 116

agriculture. See farming

alcohol, 60–61, 100

Allen County, Indiana, 99

Alsace, France, 16–19

Amana Colonies, 123

American Revolution, 20

Amish brand, 9, 89, 113, 116

Amish Farm and House (Lancaster County), 110

Amish in the City (reality series), 54, 112

Amish Mafia (reality series), 112

Amish Mennonites (19th century), 19, 23. See also Beachy Amish Mennonite affiliations

Ammann, Jakob, 15–19

Anabaptists, 14–18, 29

Andy Weaver affiliation, 37, 67

apprenticeship, 70, 75

Arcola, Illinois, 80

Arthur, Illinois, 21, 32

assimilation, 28, 108–10, 113, 117

auctions, 97

Ausbund (hymnbook), 14, 69

authority: of church, 34–35, 48, 55–56; of government, 99–102; of parents, 55–56

automobiles, 24, 26–27, 32, 58; and ownership vs. access, 1–2, 9, 33

Bann (excommunication), 17, 50–52, 55

baptism, 29; and Amish origins, 13–14, 16; described, 40–41, 49–50; and joining the Amish church, 6, 52, 55–56, 61

barn raising, 86

Bavaria, 14

Beachy, Loren, 66

Beachy Amish Mennonite affiliations, 122–23

beards, 122–23

bed courtship, 62

Beiler, David, 22

beliefs, 13–14, 29–34, 119–21

benevolence, 97

Berks County, Pennsylvania, 20

Berlin, Ohio, 98

Bible, 8, 29, 34, 48, 69, 78

birth, 44, 69, 104

birth rates, 6

bishops, 35–37, 48–49; selection of, 48

Blank, Benuel, 114–15

blood donating, 97

Bloomfield, Iowa, 101

Botschaft, Die (newspaper), 43–44

branding. See Amish brand

Breaking Amish (reality series), 112

Brethren, 123

Budget. See *Sugarcreek Budget*

buggies, 2, 33–34, 37, 99; and Slow Moving Vehicle emblems, 101. See also horse-drawn transportation

bundling. See bed courtship

bureaucracy, 7, 41–43. See also decentralization

About the Author

Steven M. Nolt is Professor of History and Senior Scholar at the Young
Center for Anabaptist and Pietist Studies at Elizabethtown College.
Recognized for his scholarship on Anabaptist groups, he is the author
or co-author of a dozen books, including the award-wining *Amish
Grace: How Forgiveness Transcended Tragedy* (with Donald Kraybill and
David Weaver-Zercher) and *The Amish* (with Donald Kraybill and
Karen Johnson-Weiner), which describes the diversity of Amish
culture in contemporary North America.